The Big Book of Sales

*Mastering The Art of Sales.
Combining powerful sales technique with an understanding of human behavior.
Build a wildly successful career in sales.
Start now!*

By
Alan Gordon

The Big Book of Sales by Alan Gordon

Published by Cycle of Mind Publishing

Sarasota, FL 34232

www.bigbookofsales.com

© 2018 Alan Gordon

All rights reserved. No portion of this book may be reproduced in any form without permission from the publisher, except as permitted by U.S. copyright law. For permissions contact:

ISBN-13: 978-1719036771

ISBN-10: 1719036772

Dedication

If you have no moral values, get out. You have no place in this profession. Sales is an ethical profession.

Over the course of my sales career I've had the opportunity to work with, learn from, and work for some of the best salespeople on the planet. I have learned so much from everyone I have met, and it is a privilege to be able to share this information with the goal of making you a more successful salesperson.

Every successful salesperson is different than the rest. They have their own personality, their own style, and their own special way of phrasing and forming sentences. But regardless of their diversity, every successful salesperson has one thing in common - confidence. They are confident because they know how to sell, and they can earn a great living. They understand that selling is a set of skills, and the more they study the details, the more successful they become.

I hope this book finds its way to the millions of hard working salesmen and saleswomen who believe in their own potential, and see a future that is better than today. You work hard, you support your family, you help your customers find a solution to their problems. Here are hundreds and hundreds of tips and techniques that I have learned from the greats through the years, and it is my privilege to share them with you now. Use this knowledge to become a better salesperson.

Nobody deserves confidence and success more than you!

Forward

My friendship with Alan Gordon began as an argument that turned into a contest. I resisted what he was telling me, but he understood what I wanted and needed and was willing to go beyond all expectations to see that I got it. I was not going to be an easy sale. The War Began!

As I objected and tried to escape, Alan patiently drew me back to the conversation. He asked targeted questions and elicited the inner desires of my heart. He saw my excuses and quietly turned me back to the benefits.

As the conversation unfolded, I began questioning my own resistance and started to pay attention. I began asking 'buyer' questions and with a smile on his face he slowly drew me closer to the end. It was effortless!

While I was resistant, he was never adversarial, he always knew that a deal would benefit both of us. There was never any high pressure or any pressure at all. It was like falling off a log. It was questions, answers, explanations, and offers. It was an amazing experience for me.

I went from a resistant and semi-angry disbeliever to a very happy and satisfied customer that was willing to buy anything this man had to offer... in about 2 short hours.

It was a Masters Degree in Sales! Experiencing that sales process with Alan was one of the most important lessons in my business life and the end result was owning his education and putting into practice some of the most sophisticated sales skills available anywhere on the planet today.

You have made a wise decision to purchase this magical book, and I would recommend you also consider his training courses. My advice would be to invest in Alan Gordon and what he can teach you about sales. You'll never look back!

This is an opportunity to change your life by learning how to sell. It's a skill you will use forever and at a cost of a fast food lunch.

Buy the Big Book of Sales, join the membership program, read, study and apply what you learn, and you will be set for life. It's that simple.

I wish you the best!

Charles W. Rolfe

Thank You For Investing in this Book! It is my sincere hope that you will take the powerful information contained in the book and build your confidence as a salesperson and have an amazing sales career. You deserve success!

As a reward for making this investment I also have a Free Gift for You:

Get a free one month membership in our Big Book of Sales online community! Inside this membership you will find lots of free goodies and some really helpful videos and tools. Enjoy!

To grab your reward and take a look at some of our video training courses

Just CLICK HERE or visit https://www.bigbookofsales.com.

If you would like to buy this book in bulk for your entire sales team, or would like sales training customized for your company, please email

specialrequest@bigbookofsales.com.

Thanks!

Alan

Table of Contents

Dedication iii

Forward... iv

Introduction - The Key to Becoming a Master Salesman........................ 1

Everyone is in Sales - Whether They Know it or Not 4

Mastering the Sales Platform 9

The Reality of Sales - Nothing is Given to You – You Earn Everything... 11

Influence 13

Needs Development Questions 17

Building Value 25

Who is the Decision Maker?... 30

Features vs. Benefits - Remember the Six Magic Words in Sales 37

What that means to you is… 39

Add ENTHUSIASM to Your Pitch 40

Capturing Your Customer's FULL Attention... 45

A Disarming Sales Approach - Because People Buy From
People They Like.. 48

Things Every Salesman Should Know 51

Implicit Agreement / Tag Questions 55

Green Light, Yellow Light, Red Light 58

The Pattern Interrupt.. 61

Implied Questions 63

The Embarrassed Questions 65

Future Tense - Imagine What it Will Be Like 66

Reflecting and Paraphrasing 68
Question Technique - Probe and Clarify.. 72
Improve the Quality of Your Questions 76
Exploratory Questions - The "Key and Pivot" Technique 78
Moving Past the Putoff 83
Getting the Appointment - Getting in to Meet With Them 85
Get Them Physically Involved 92
Tie the "New" to the "Old" - Habit Theory 93
References and Validation 96
The 45 Second Rule 98
The Trial Close - Find Out Where You Stand 99
Handling Objections - Here's the Right Way to Do it........................... 103
Flipping the BUT - Help Them Resolve Their Concerns 114
Loss Statements Can Save a Sale 119
The Price Objection - It's Really a Buying Signal.................................. 123
Let Me Think it Over 126
Practice Makes Perfect - Handling Objections Like a Pro 128
I Need to Talk About This With My Partner 131
Questions and Tie-Downs - Questions Are a Sign of Interest 136
"We're Not Buying Today" - How to Handle This Situation 139
The Psychological Pin Down 151
Closing Techniques - Three Closes Are All You Will Ever Need............ 153
One More Closing Technique - "Here's What's Going
to Happen Next." 158
Creating Urgency - How Can We Get Them to Buy Today?................. 160
Submitting a Bid or Proposal - Last is Best.. 168
Putting it All Together With an Example: 171

Cold Calling 176
   Cold Calling - Adjust Your Attitude 179
   Cold Calling - Realistic Goals for the Cold Call 181
   Cold Calling - A Step by Step Plan 184
   Cold Calling - Leaving a Voice Message 185
   Cold Calling - Crafting a Concise Opening Statement 189
   Cold Calling - Handling Control Statements 193
   Cold Calling - Example 195

Different Types of Sales 201
   Selling to Consumers in Their Home 202
   Selling to Consumers in a Store 206
   Selling to Businesses by Phone 209
   Selling to Corporations or Large Groups 212
   Self-Evaluation After Every Call 218
   How to Work a Trade Show Booth 220
   The Trade Show "Bounce" 222
   Attitude, Hard Work and Self-Motivation 226
   How Do You Fell About Money and Success? 229
   Becoming a Great Sales Manager 233

BONUS SECTIONS 239
   Listening - Reaching the Unconscious to Gain Positive Influence ... 240
   The Conscious Mind vs. The Unconscious Mind 248
   Body Language and Non-Verbal Communication 251
   Circumstances That Influence 254
   Words That Influence 259
   Suggestions and Embedded Commands 263

Introduction

The Key to Becoming a Master Salesman

There's an old saying that *selling is like fishing*. The more hooks you put in the water, the more fish you catch.

That's true, but I'm going to take that analogy in a different direction because selling really is like fishing – but in a completely different way.

When I go fishing I can spend six hours on the lake and not get a single nibble, let alone catch any fish. You've seen these TV shows about fishing, and how they follow world class fishermen as they go out on the lake and catch fish. These guys stop the boat at a certain site, drop a line in the water and in less than two minutes they're bringing a fish on board. I always wondered how that was possible.

What's the difference between these professionals and me? Even if I had the exact same boat and the same equipment, why can they catch multiple fish in 30 minutes, and I can go all day and get nothing?

Here's why.

Because when I drive my boat on a lake, all I see is the top of the lake. I have no idea what's going on under the water. To me this spot is as good as any other spot.

A professional fisherman has a totally different view. He understands how the fish live. How they make their little burrows at the bottom. How the different species interact, what they like to eat, what time they eat, where they like to hang out, how they interact with other fish.

A professional knows everything about his equipment (the boat, the rod and reel, the lures), **but he also knows everything about the fish**. He knows exactly what they like and how they behave.

If I was foolish enough to enter a fishing contest against a professional fisherman I would have no chance. We can use the same boat, the same rod and reel, the same lures – but I can never beat him. I'm seeing the surface of the lake while he's understanding the whole fish population in that lake, the terrain on the bottom of the lake, and how all the fish interact with their environment and each other. He's sensing the temperature, the clouds, the angle of the sun, the time of day and he understands things that I don't even know exist.

The boat, the rod and reel, the lures – those are the tools you need to fish.

Salespeople have their own tools - the cold call, the needs development process, the presentation, the trial close, handling objections, closing. You need to be an expert at using these sales tools. For the most part, sales training focuses on these tools. There's no substitute for learning, memorizing, practicing and perfecting these tools.

> **But to be a master at the art of sales, you also need to understand how your customers buy,** how they react to salespeople, how they process information, and how they make a decision. As you're selling you are on the surface of the lake. If you can understand what's happening under the surface, if you can understand your customer's thought process and behaviors – then you actually start to see why sales tools work, and how they work. When you combine an understanding of customer behavior with a precise execution of your sales skills you will be on your way to mastering your profession.

As an example, when a customer says "Let me think this over," that means NO SALE to most salespeople. But I love it when a customer says he wants to think it over – I'm counting my commission when I hear that – because I understand what this response means in the mind of the customer as he is going through his decision process (knowledge of customer behavior). But equally important, I know exactly what to say next in that situation (knowledge of the sales technique). Let Me Think It Over.

When you combine strong sales technique with an understanding of customer behavior – now you're selling. Add a strong work ethic and you might make some money on this job!

Does a professional fisherman catch every fish? No. But his knowledge of the equipment <u>combined with</u> his knowledge of the fish's behavior dramatically increases his odds over the amateur.

Everyone is in Sales

Whether They Know it or Not

You've heard the theory that everyone is in sales. Regardless of our job or profession, we all have to present our ideas and influence others. Even just being a parent or a husband or a wife puts you in situations where you need to communicate and influence.

Selling is a set of skills designed to communicate and influence. There are people who are naturally good at selling, but we can all learn these skills if we apply ourselves to the task.

Everyone is engaged in communicating and influencing.

We really are all in sales. An Accountant could gain more clients if he learned how to sell. A lawyer could win more cases if he learned how to sell. An exterminator, carpet cleaner, landscaper would all get more customers if they learned how to sell. A handyman could get more projects if he learned how to sell. But understandably, they don't think of themselves as salespeople and they don't want to learn how to sell.

I thought of naming this book: The Big Book of Communication and Influence.

Everyone is engaged in selling every day, but they will not call themselves salespeople. They do not want to learn how to sell.

But salespeople are different. Salespeople, unlike so many others who would benefit from knowing sales skills, but don't want to learn them – salespeople take the time to prepare, memorize, improve and perfect their communication and influence skills.

> Selling is nothing more than asking questions to uncover a customer's needs, presenting ideas or services in a way which meets those needs, being able to skillfully address questions, concerns and objections the customer brings up, and moving the discussion to a successful close and an ongoing relationship.
>
> **On top of that**, layer an understanding of human psychology, and an ability to influence the customer's thinking and decision making – and that's the complete sales process. Sales is the art of communication and influence.
>
> **On top of THAT**, layer your own unique personality then grab the skills that work for your personality. Then identify your weaknesses, and diligently work on strengthening those weak areas until you become a sales master, the best salesman you can be.

I understand why an Accountant would never call himself a salesperson – he's an Accountant. But the fact is, when a potential client calls in and wants to talk to the Accountant about his services, that potential client either signs up as a client, or he dials the next phone number and interviews the next Accountant. However, if that Accountant took the time to learn the sales process, to learn the steps within each process, to learn the skills and techniques of influence, and to learn and practice his words and phrases – that Accountant would have a lot more customers. His Accounting practice would be more successful.

You Are a Professional Salesperson – Regardless of What You Sell

Professional salespeople are engaged in thousands of different selling scenarios. Every salesperson is different and every sales situation is different, but all sales involve the art and skill of communication and influence.

Selling appliances to couples in an appliance store is a very different process than selling a $300,000 software package to a large corporation, or a $5,000,000 outsourcing arrangement to a Fortune 100 financial institution. The appliance salesman needs to understand how couples interact, what drives them to buy, and how they make a decision. The software salesman needs to understand how C-Level executives interact and what methods they use to evaluate the impact of a $300,000 piece of software. The outsourcing salesman needs to have an understanding of bank operations, and the larger economic forces impacting technology, process and labor trends.

The appliance salesman may make 6 to 10 sales in a day. The software salesman may sell five software packages in a year. The outsourcing salesman may be assigned to a single account and take two years to sell his client an outsourcing program.

> Every salesperson and sales situation is different, but no matter how different their sales processes may be, they all need to understand how to communicate and influence.
>
> That's what this book is about!
>
> All salesmen use the same skills, but each selling situation is different, and you need to not only master and perfect the skills involved in the sales process, but you also need to understand how the customers in your industry behave.

Adapt the Sales Skills in This Book to Your Situation

It's obvious, but I'll say it anyway. Everything you read in this book needs to be adapted to your situation. Some ideas and techniques will be perfect for your type of sale, while others won't apply to your situation at all. Also, some techniques may fit perfectly with your personality, while other techniques are not a good match. **Use your brain and adapt all the skills in this book to your situation.** Regardless of the type of sale you are engaged in, or your personality type, there is plenty in this book for you – you just need to apply it to your situation.

Improving sales skills is a lifelong process. Think of selling as a skill you are constantly improving, as a profession, not a job. Improvement is a never ending process.

The key to improving your sales skills is to try one new skill at a time, try it out, and see if you can become comfortable with that skill. An open mind, a willingness to try new ideas, and a long term view of your improvement will serve you well as you grow your sales skills.

In the moment of a sales call you will always revert back to the skills you are comfortable with. The key to growing is to continually add new skills and over time expand your comfort zone, so in the heat of a sales call you will have more tools and more skills to fall back on.

There is no one book you can read (not even this book), or one thing I can teach you, or one class you can attend to make you a great salesperson. There are many things, and learning these techniques takes years as you learn a new skill, and then incorporate it into your day to day sales work. Each month, each year you become more experienced, more confident in a variety of situations, and you become more successful.

Your growth as a sales professional is measured in years. Everyone is different, some people pick up certain skills quickly, others take more time to adapt their style. The better you are, the faster you are able to pick up and incorporate new skills. The better you are, the more powerful each new skill becomes – like putting a new tool in the hands of a master – you know exactly what to do with it.

There is no book that will make you great in one day. Each book and each training session offers you one or two new ideas which give you a new perspective, and one or two new skills you can apply on your next calls.

This book is intended to be read often. Each time through you will pick up a new skill to incorporate into your daily selling. Some of these skills are very basic communication techniques or phrases you can use – others will change your perspective and help you sell at a higher level.

So Here's My Pet Peeve

Just like you, I've read a hundred sales books. I HATE books that are vague and general. As you will see in the coming chapters, I always try to give real sentences you can use or adapt to your specific situation.

Sales, at its core, is about increasing the sophistication of your communication skills, becoming comfortable with new words and phrases, becoming comfortable asking questions at the right time, having an awareness of your customer's psychology in the moment, then having the experience and courage to use the necessary skill at the right moment.

So without further ado – let's learn some skills!

Mastering the Sales Platform

If you ever watch a great hitter come to home plate, he takes his time. The on-deck circle, the home plate area, the batter's box – this is his "work area", this is where he earns his living. Sure he plays in the outfield, but everyone knows that home plate is where this man earns his paycheck.

The bat, the pine tar, the batting gloves – these are his tools. All his past experiences, the thousands of hours of batting practice, the film study, the pre-game meetings – he brings all of this to the plate.

He usually only gets four at-bats in a game against the best pitchers in the world, and he also knows during those four at-bats he may only see one good pitch. He is looking for that one pitch he can "drive".

When a great hitter steps into the batter's box he is ready. He knows the situation. He understands the pitcher – his strengths and weaknesses and his tendencies. He takes his time. He is completely alert, aware of everything, and knows exactly what to expect in every situation. He anticipates. There is nothing this pitcher can throw at him that he won't be ready for. He isn't going to hit a home run every time, but he will make the most of every opportunity.

In the same way, salespeople have what I call a Sales Platform – it's like Home Plate for salespeople. The Sales Platform is that moment when you are meaningfully engaged with a prospect. This is your batter's box. This is your "work area", and when your time comes you need to be ready, alert, prepared, and anticipating all possible situations.

You may have the kind of sales job where you get 10 or 15 shots at a Sales Platform every day, or it may take you a hundred phone calls to get only one shot at it, or in high level corporate sales you may have a month of planning for the "big meeting". However often you get an "at bat", you need to be completely prepared and ready for everything.

Anything less than 100% preparation would be shortchanging yourself and those who depend on you and expect you to be great.

The Reality of Sales

Nothing is Given to You – You Earn Everything

With the advent of the internet in the early 1990's it was predicted that salespeople would soon be obsolete. People will buy on the web and will never need to talk to a salesperson. And people do buy on the web, to the tune of $100B each year and growing. But the need for salespeople has not gone away. In some industries the role of the salesperson has changed, but in fact the need for high quality, relationship oriented salespeople is stronger than ever. In addition, small local businesses continue to need salespeople to grow their business. Small business owners need to learn how to sell.

A company's website can generate leads, advertisements can generate incoming traffic, but someone still needs to talk to the customer, find out what they are looking for, and help them navigate through the sales process to the completed transaction.

People still buy from people, and until that changes salespeople with a mature sales communication skill set will continue to be essential to a large number of businesses.

Through a series of incremental steps, a salesperson moves a prospect through each of the following phases, eventually converting new prospects into customers, and then repeat customers.

Cold Call → Warm Call → Transaction → Relationship → Repeat Relationship

Salespeople put themselves in a position to meet targeted prospects and are able to navigate the first few seconds of a cold call introduction. After a minute of conversation, the meeting becomes a warm call, hopefully leading to a transaction. After conducting business together, the prospect becomes a customer and a relationship now exists. When the salesperson follows up with the customer, he deepens the relationship and develops a repeat relationship.

When you are hired into a new sales position, the other salespeople already have the best customers, and I haven't met a salesperson yet who is willing to give the new sales rep their best relationship customers. When you start a new sales position, you start at the bottom because nobody gives you anything. You are going to cold call, and you will sink or swim on the new job based almost entirely on your ability to convert cold calls to warm calls to transactions to relationships.

Here's the reality. A sales manager is not going to give the best leads to you. He's going to give them to the sales reps he knows have the best chance at converting them into sales. Until you build your own track record, you're not going to get anything handed to you. Once you give a reason for your sales manager to have confidence in you, the good leads will start coming.

Count it as a rare blessing if you are given warm leads, or customers who already have a relationship with your company. For the most part, you're going to have to Cold Call if you want your first commission check.

As you learn the skills presented in this book, you will begin to have success. When you succeed, you become more valuable to the company, and you will be given more opportunities. Have confidence, continually work on improving your skills, and work your butt off! You can do it!

Influence

In my early days of sales I used to think my role as a salesman was to lay out all the details of my product or service, help the customer understand all his options, and then allow the customer to come to his own conclusion about moving forward with my company. I didn't feel it was appropriate for me to influence a customer. If it was right for them, they would recognize it and move forward with me. If it was not right for them, they would not. My role was to give them all the information they needed to make the right decision. I was there to inform and educate, not influence.

I defined this behavior as "ethical." I felt that sales methods or tactics were unethical. I felt that influencing people one way or the other was unethical. This is the main reason why many people (who would make great salespeople) don't want to be in sales, or don't respect sales as a profession. They feel that salespeople are pushy, and that influencing is unethical – they don't want to do it.

Normally, if a salesperson does not understand influence techniques, or refuses to try to influence customers, they tend to be unsuccessful and quickly move out of sales. However, I was very fortunate to have met, worked with, and worked for many good and great sales professionals who took the time to teach me, work with me, critique me and talk with me about selling for hours.

They showed me all their secrets, all their techniques, and it is because I have received so much help in my own career, that I have developed the attitude of helping other salespeople. I would do anything to help another salesperson, and I would never ask them for anything in return. I just want salespeople to become better at what they do, to be successful, and to make more money.

Throughout this book I share hundreds of techniques to influence your customers, and I know many salespeople may shy away from these techniques because it makes them feel uncomfortable – they don't want to be pushy. I know exactly how they feel, and why they feel this way because, earlier in my own sales career, I felt the same way.

I also know that there are many salespeople who feel that being an "advisor" or a "consultant" is the true nature of the profession. Your job is to uncover more information about the customer and his or her unique situation, identify opportunities and then act as a partner to share the best solutions with them. To these salespeople, old fashioned sales methods are worn and out of date. Influencing is out, educating is in.

I actually agree with everyone. The truth is, there are hundreds of different sales jobs – some selling direct to consumers, others selling business to business. Some involve retail selling in a store, others involve calling on corporate executives with an 18 month sales cycle, and everything in between.

There is no single sales method that will work in every sales situation, but there are three things that every salesperson must master:

- The ability to question, listen and understand,
- The ability to communicate effectively, and
- The ability to persuade and influence to a close.

If you believe that one or two of these is important, but not the other, you are greatly limiting your potential as a sales professional. All three components are critical.

At some point I had a change of perspective, and it dawned on me that influence is not unethical. It is a natural activity. As one example, and there are many, when you go on a job interview you dress professionally. You probably don't wear a suit and tie every day, but for the interview you dress up to impress your potential employer. You are trying to influence them to hire you. There is nothing wrong with attempting to influence. I would expect you to put your best foot forward. I would expect you to tell me all your positive qualities, and I would not expect you to start listing all the reasons why the other candidates for the job might be better.

In the exact same way, when you first meet a potential customer you must present your product or service, your company, yourself, in the most positive light. Not as a way to deceive or coerce the customer, but to get the customer to join with hundreds or thousands of already satisfied customers. You want them to work with you. You want them to join with your other customers to get the benefit of your product or service. You want to include them as one of your customers.

Your job is to listen to the customer's unique situation and needs to determine if your product or service is a fit, and if so then your job is to use your expertise to help guide the customer through the sales process of learning, evaluating, and deciding to move forward.

As salespeople, YES WE DO WANT TO INFLUENCE OUR CUSTOMERS. We want to influence them to like us. We want to influence them to trust us. We want to influence them to work with us (rather than the many competing companies and solutions out there). We want to influence them to decide and move forward. Move forward with us – of course.

As long as the company you work for is ethical, and the product or service you offer is of good quality at a fair price, then all the techniques you use to influence your customers, to gain market share, to grow your company, and to grow your own salary are completely ethical. You want to become an expert in the art of influence, not to manipulate customers, but to have them choose you, choose your product, choose your company.

When I refused to use influencing techniques, I did ok, but I lost many customers who should have worked with me. It was not good for them, not good for my company, and certainly not good for me personally.

> As a salesperson it is your job, your mission to influence as many customers as possible to work with you, to work with your company, to help your company grow, to help your company gain market share.
>
> This is not only ethical, it is your professional obligation.

So without further ado, prepare to learn hundreds of simple (and some advanced) secrets that salespeople are using every day to listen, to understand their customers, to influence, and to sell.

Needs Development Questions

Needs Development is the single most important section in this book. It is the single most important sales skill. If you're not doing Needs Development, and then you start doing it – you will wonder how you ever sold anything before. Needs Development questions (also referred to as Discovery) help you dig into what the customer actually needs, dig into his individual circumstances. Obviously, the more you know about the customer's individual needs, the better you can position your solution.

Very often, a customer will begin the conversation by asking a specific question or for a specific item. An inexperienced salesperson will answer the specific question or explain the specific item requested. But if you pause for a second and get the bigger picture, as you work through your needs development questions, you usually discover that the customer is actually interested in something completely different, or this may be only a small part of a very large project.

There are so many benefits to asking Needs Development questions:

- Understand a customer's specific circumstances – no two customers are the same
- Get information about what the customer is thinking
- Have the customer prioritize what is most important to them
- Understand what your customer values

- Customize your presentation to what is important to them
- Qualify the opportunity
- Find out who you're competing with
- Gain credibility as an expert
- Build your relationship with the customer because you are showing them the respect of asking them questions then listening to their answers

When you combine the process of Needs Development and genuinely listening to their answers (and asking more questions), it makes a customer feel comfortable with you, and often times they stop looking elsewhere. Because you have taken a little time to listen to them before you start diving into your presentation, they gain confidence that you understand them and can take care of their needs.

No matter what you're selling, you should develop a list of Needs Development questions, and they should flow naturally early in the call.

Needs Development questions should cover the following:
- Fact finding – gathering information
- Qualifying the opportunity
- Goals / plans / future
- Past experiences
- Priorities – what's most important
- Concerns / problems / issues
- Competitive situation

By asking good questions you start to understand the customer's needs. He won't care about every feature in your product or service, but you can find out which will be the most important to him and show him how your solution addresses his specific situation and priorities.

The more information you gather, the more your solution can focus on his exact needs.

I can't tell you how many times in my life a salesperson has just dove into their presentation and I (or my wife) has had to stop them. *"We don't travel very often." "Our children are already out of school." "We're moving in a few months." "We already have life insurance."* They never bothered to ask us even the most basic questions before they started telling us how great their product is.

Examples of Needs Development Questions

LIFE INSURANCE

How much life insurance do you have now?
Is it Whole Life or Term Insurance?
What do you think would be the right amount?
Are any of your other family members insured?
When is the last time you reviewed your insurance?
What are your goals?
What is most important to you?
What is your biggest concern?
How is your health? Are there any recent changes in your health?
How many years do you think you want to keep working before you retire?
What life changes have taken place since you last purchased insurance?
How important would a Double Indemnity Rider be to you?
Tell me how your life insurance plan needs to interact with your overall financial plan.

EXTERMINATOR
How often do you see bugs in your home?

When was the last time you inspected for termites?
What areas of your home specifically concern you?
When was the last time you actually talked to your current pest control company?
What outside areas have you seen a problem with?
What is most important to you?
What are your expectations from a pest control company?
How often do you get your lawn treated for pest control?

REAL ESTATE AGENT

What type of home are you interested in?
How many children do you have?
Do you have any pets?
Where do you work?
How long do you want your commute?
What are your goals?
What is your biggest concern?
Would you rather live in a rural area, suburban, or closer to a city?
How important is the school district you're in?
What activities are you and your children involved in?
What type of floor plan do you think best suits your family?
How often do you entertain?
Do you have other family members who will be staying with you from time to time?
What's the single most important factor in choosing the right home?

HEALTH CLUB MEMBERSHIP

Tell me about your fitness goals.
What's the main reason you want to join a health club?
Are you recovering from an injury or illness?
Have you ever been a member of another health club?
What did you like about it? What didn't you like?

What parts of your body are you most interested in developing?
What do you think is the biggest weakness in your health plan?
Have you ever used a personal trainer?
Do you like group classes, or do you prefer to work out on your own?

Salesman A just starts walking the prospective customer through the health club without asking these questions. He gives the same tour to everyone and half of what he's showing isn't even of interest to them.

Salesman B sits for a few quick minutes to ask these questions (sometimes leading to other questions), and learns about this person's specific circumstances. Now he can guide the customer through the health club – emphasizing all the things they said were most important.

Which salesperson do you think has the better chance of selling the membership?

SELLING SOFTWARE AND HARDWARE
Tell me a little about your IT environment.
Do you outsource IT management, or manage it yourself?
What type of network equipment do you use?
When are you planning your next upgrade? What will you be upgrading?
What business issues are driving you to change/improve your IT?
What are your goals?
What is your biggest concern?
What is the most important priority?
How much do you have budgeted for this project?
Help me understand your budget process.
Tell me a little about your decision process?
What applications are you running?
What type of servers do you purchase?
Who is your current vendor?

Do you always purchase new, or have you ever used refurbished equipment?
Have you put this out to other companies for a quote? Who's got the inside track?
What are the implications if you lose your data?
How often have you been experiencing downtime?
Who do you currently purchase equipment from?
What are the most important attributes when you consider an equipment vendor?

TIRES

How many miles do you drive in a year?
How much of your driving is local and how much long distance?
What kind of tires do you have on your car now?
How many years are you planning to keep your car?
Who's driving this car? Is it you or your wife or one of your children?
How important is safety when you choose your tires?
Would you consider spending a little more for safer tires, or do you just want the cheapest ones?
Do you have any brand preference when you buy tires?
Do you get your tires balanced every time you have your oil changed?

BUSINESS BROKER

Selling your business is obviously a very important step...
What's driving you to sell now?
What are the most important things you want to accomplish by selling now?
What are your personal goals?
What is your biggest concern about selling your business?
When you make a final decision, what will be the most important factors?
How does your wife feel about you selling the business?

How closely do you want to be involved with the new management after the sale?
Do you have employees you want to safeguard after the sale?
What assets are included in the sale?
How did you arrive at an asking price?

APPLIANCES
How many loads of laundry do you do in a week?
How many children do you have?
What's your main complaint with the machine you have now?
Do you have a brand preference?
Do you want front load or top load?
How important is saving water and electricity – being green?
Are we matching these to any other appliances?
Have you already gotten pricing from the internet or another appliance store?
What's most important to you?

Notice that you haven't said a single word about your product or service, but you know a lot about their situation, their needs, their motivations, their priorities, their budget, and how decisions are made.

It's very important that you have your own set of Needs Development questions. Periodically take a look at your list of questions and revise them and add better questions.

All these questions lead to more questions.

This is the single most important difference between top salespeople and average salespeople. Top salespeople ask questions, then ask more questions, then ask more questions.

Never present a solution until you know as much as possible about the customer, his situation, his needs, his priorities, his past experiences, his decision process, the competitive situation, etc.

Most salespeople just give their pitch. Great salespeople ask questions to uncover more and more detail about a customer's situation. Then they tailor their solution to meet the customer's needs exactly.

Building Value

Here is the best definition of Value I have been able to put together:

Value is the direct linking of your product's / service's unique benefits to the most important needs and desires of the customer.

Value is the link between what your customer needs/wants, and what your product/service does. Furthermore, if you are selling to more than one person you'll almost always find they have different needs/wants, and therefore what is valuable to one person may not be valuable to others in the group.

Value is a critical element in all sales situations regardless of the product or service you're selling. Regardless of your target customers – from a husband and wife buying a living room set to a large corporation investing in complex business software - if your customer does not see the value, they won't buy. Conversely, if they see the value, they will be happy to buy.

Salespeople tend to think in terms of their product and its features. They are product experts.

But great salespeople are "customer value" experts.

How do you find out what your customer values? You have to ASK. Needs Development.

Here are a few examples.

When you go to buy a car, you might be focused on the price – but it is just as likely that you are focused on prestige, or safety, or the warranty, or performance, or even the color of the car. As it turns out, price may not be the primary need/desire.

Your job, through Needs Development Questions, is to determine the customer's primary needs and desires – then show them exactly how "this car" (not every other car on the lot) meets their needs exactly. Add to the situation that a husband may have a completely different set of priorities than the wife, or that the teenage son may have a completely different set of priorities than his parents, so while you're selling performance and the 'smokin' sound system to the son, you're selling safety and warranty to the parents.

If you properly link the features of the car to their individual needs and desires, the car will literally pull them in. It's exactly what they wanted when they walked in the door.

Suppose you're selling tires in a tire store. Everyone who walks into your store mentions the ad in the newspaper – buy 3 get 1 free. These are the cheapest tires. By asking a few Needs Development questions (as listed in the previous chapter) you can get them into the best tires for their situation. Maybe the cheapest tires are best for them, but maybe they would benefit from safer and longer lasting tires, and then you can encourage them to get an alignment – a great investment because it reduces wear on the tires and they will last longer. All these upgrades are better for the customer, and you turned a $300 sale into a $600 sale. Don't just give them what they want, find out what they NEED.

When a Real Estate Agent works with a couple, she must first completely understand the needs of both partners. Is it commute time? Status? Neighborhood? School District? Square footage? Closet size? Color? Architectural style? Or something else?

A Real Estate Agent has to sell certain features to the husband, and possibly a completely different set of features to the wife.

If you're selling corporate sponsorships for a baseball team, find out what are the most important issues for that CEO. Is it the opportunity to entertain his clients? Is it the VIP service in the Suite? Is it the company's name on the center field fence? Is he going to bring his children to the games? Is it the free parking and the other perks that corporate sponsors get? Is it access to the clubhouse and meeting the players after the game?

Before you start rattling off all the benefits of a corporate sponsorship, wouldn't it be best to do some discovery and find out what this CEO most highly values? Find out what will get him interested.

If you do your Needs Development properly and thoroughly, creating value becomes much easier. And you will find that **Value Trumps Price** almost every time. In fact, value must trump price, otherwise only the cheapest company would survive in the market – but we all know that many companies survive in every market, because cheapest is not always best. Cheapest is not always what the customer needs.

Develop Your Unique Value Proposition

If you are not the cheapest solution, then start by asking what makes your product or service unique? Why would a customer buy this product – what problem does it solve? Why is your product or service different than the many other options your customers have? Then ask yourself why would a customer pay extra for that unique feature or service? What value does my product or service bring to the customer?

You may be selling a commodity product or service. They can get the same thing from a hundred different providers. Why should they buy it from you instead of anyone else?

Value may lie in the product or service itself, it may lie in the price, it may lie in your company and its reputation for service, or it may lie in you as the salesperson. Each of these areas needs to be explored.

Value is not just the benefits of your product or service, it's the benefits as they relate to the issues and concerns your customer is facing. That's why the Needs Development process is so critical. The more you understand about your customer's business, their challenges, their issues, their needs, their concerns, their fears, their hopes, their dreams – the more you can build up the value of your solution.

Tie Your Needs Development Questions to Your Unique Strengths

Build your Needs Development questions specifically to include your areas of strength vs. the competition. If you have the cheapest solution your questions should hammer away at keeping the cost down. If you are more expensive, but you have better service your questions should build the case for service, support, warranty by probing for negative experiences where the cheapest ended up being a disaster because of poor quality and service.

If you're a CPA and you're cold calling potential clients, ask questions like:

> "When is the last time you and your CPA sat down and reviewed your goals?"
> "When is the last time you reviewed your annual tax plan? Wow! You don't have an annual tax plan?"
> "How important is a personal relationship with your CPA?"
> "What else is important in your relationship with your CPA?"

Now you are in a great position to match your commitment to personal "first name basis" service to your customer's needs and desires. Even if it turns out that your service is more expensive than what they are currently paying, they will see the value in your personal level of service – "which might save you tens of thousands of dollars in the next year, because even though it may take us quite a bit of digging, we are constantly looking for strategies that apply to your specific situation."

Value trumps price.

The key to real selling is to understand the problems and issues your customers face, their fears, worries and concerns, their wants and desires, and match them – one by one – to how your solution directly addresses these issues.

Through carefully planned Needs Development Questions, an advanced salesperson can subtly guide a customer to prioritize their values in such a way that they match the strengths of his or her solution.

Who is the Decision Maker?

Avoid the Trap

One of the biggest traps salespeople fall into is to give their presentation (and submit their proposal) to a person who is not the decision maker.

With my wife and I, depending on what we're shopping for, sometimes I am the decision maker, and sometimes my wife is the one who needs to be convinced. You can talk to me all you want about furniture or artwork or anything related to our home - but I'm not the one you have to sell. And vice versa on other issues. You can convince her all you want, but if I'm not convinced - no sale.

If you don't understand the decision process, you will lose far more often than you win.

> Most salespeople don't uncover the decision process because they are uncomfortable asking these questions up front.

(Read on to see examples of these types of questions).

However, once you understand the concept of "selling to power", you realize that it makes no sense to move the sales process forward without knowing where the decision power lies. So this becomes one of the most significant factors separating top performers from average performers.

With a husband and wife, or a small business with only a few employees, it is very easy to avoid the trap of presenting to the wrong person.

Early in the process simply ask, and they will tell you.

"How do you normally make a decision like this?"

Don't ask "Who is the decision maker?" because they may not tell you, or they may simply tell you that they are the decision maker. It is better to ask the open-ended question which invites more discussion and more follow-up questions about their decision process.

Once you understand the decision process and who the decision maker is, don't ignore the non-decision maker. Just the opposite, you still need to make both people feel comfortable with your product or service - but once you understand who the decision maker is, you are in position to determine their decision criteria.

More Complex in Larger Corporations

In longer term B2B sales, the situation is far more complicated. Selling to a non-decision maker can cost you weeks and even months of effort.

In larger corporations, the days are gone when every department had its own budget. Over the last ten years, financial controls have consolidated decision making at a higher level. As one Regional VP said, "I'm sorry for the long decision process. A few years ago I could have approved this amount ten times over. Now I need permission to buy a Coke."

For any significant purchase, there is normally a group (formal or informal) who will evaluate your product / service, and provide their input and opinion to the decision maker. But remember, if the decision maker does not understand the value of the solution - no sale.

Here are some different roles you may run into in larger corporations:

The Internal Champion

This person is receptive to your solution. They are open and up front throughout the process. They ask great questions. They give you all the requirements. They answer your phone calls.

> As salespeople we LOVE talking to the internal champion. We submit our proposals and just sit back and count our commissions. They love me. They love my solution. This is in the bag.
>
> Unfortunately your champion is not the decision maker.

Sometimes your internal champion will take your proposal through the process and win the deal for you. Unfortunately, because this sometimes works, average salespeople continue this low-performance strategy.

If you are happy closing one out of every five proposals, then you can continue with this strategy. If you would like to double or triple your close / proposal ratio, then you will need to learn to use your internal champion to open up the decision process and get you to the rest of the stakeholders, including the decision maker.

When a salesperson has a lower than average win rate on their quotes - this is almost always the reason.

Another way to look at it is if you want to improve your win-rate on quotes and proposals, then the surest way to do this is to locate the decision maker early in the process, discover their needs and criteria, and ensure that your proposal specifically addresses their needs.

Stakeholders and Influencers

You would think that the people / organizations affected by the purchase (stakeholders) are the ones who get to decide on the purchase. This is often not true. Quite often, these stakeholders are part of the evaluation team, but the decision maker is not a direct stakeholder.

Because of differing personalities and organizational dynamics, each stakeholder has a different level of influence. Some are very influential, while others are involved in the process, but don't have much of a voice in the final decision.

You need to understand the needs of all the stakeholders, and to build value with each of them, but also recognize the dynamics of power and decision making.

The Financial Analyst

There is normally at least one person in the decision making process who doesn't really care about the merits of any of the proposals. He or she is most concerned with bottom line price - they are looking at the expense. They measure each proposal by its cost, not by the benefit it brings to the stakeholder organizations.

> *"We simply can't afford to do this right now."*
> *"There are less expensive ways to solve this problem."*
> *"We should choose the lowest price quote."*

It is always best to include the expense-minded person in your presentation so you can address their expense concerns up front. Ways to address their concerns are to look at the savings your product/service will generate vs. their current situation, new revenue the product/service will generate, internal improvements, credit and payment terms which allow them to spread the cost over several years, etc.

If you do not include the Financial Analyst in your process, they often will shoot your proposal down when the internal champion presents your solution to them.

The Decision Maker

The person making the final decision is not always the CEO. Often times the CEO may not be involved. They may have handed their decision making authority over to someone else (formally or informally), or your project is not big enough to hit their radar. If you find out who the decision maker is, you can take steps to find out their main concerns, and deal with their questions and objections to your proposal. If you have not identified the decision maker, then you are not able to address their concerns in your proposal, and so your proposal has a much lower chance of success when it is finally presented to them.

Once you discover the needs and priorities of the decision maker, your proposal immediately has the "inside track," and the "inside track" is definitely the place to be.

The decision maker has his/her own unique set of needs and requirements. If they decide yes, they overrule the Financial Analyst, and the money will be spent. If they decide no, they overrule the stakeholder organizations, and the solution will not get implemented – their problem will remain unresolved.

Be Aggressive Early in the Process

Here are some examples of questions you can ask to your internal champion to open up their decision process and help you gain access to all the stakeholders and the decision maker.

> "Can you walk me through your decision process?"
>
> "How does your company go about making an important decision like this?"
>
> "Who has the final signoff on this decision?"
>
> "Who are the major stakeholders in this decision?"
>
> "What other organizations or people are affected by this decision?"

"Who's budget is this project coming from?"

"Who controls the budget to pay for this?"

"Our process works best when we can get all the stakeholders in the room (or on the phone) together to make sure that our proposal includes the needs of everyone involved. How can we arrange that to happen?"

"I want to create a proposal that is comprehensive. How can I find out the specific concerns of all the people who will be involved in this decision?"

"Do you always choose the lowest cost proposal?"

"No"

"OK then what other criteria besides price do you use?"

"It has to meet our needs."

"OK great. How do we get everyone in the room together so we can get a complete list of everyone's needs?"

What to Do if You Get Stonewalled

Sometimes, despite your best efforts, your internal champion is also a Gatekeeper. They play their cards close to the vest, and are simply not going to allow you to meet with the decision maker. They may not even identify the decision maker. You have to present the information to them, and they will take it up the ladder.

You can walk away and refuse to present.

"I'm sure you can understand that our process works best when we meet with all the stakeholders, so that our proposal can address all their concerns."

But still no luck.

Here's what you do next.

"I understand your process. All the vendors present their solution to you, then you present the solutions to the stakeholders. That certainly makes sense. So let me ask you, what are the key concerns of the different stakeholders and the decision maker? What are the criteria they will use to evaluate and rank each vendor's proposal?"

This is another way to try to get at the needs of the evaluation team and the decision maker. Of course, it is not as effective as speaking with them personally, but at least you can make an effort to get a broader view beyond the gatekeeper. This approach also allows you to continue to ask more and more questions about the requirements and evaluation criteria.

Features vs. Benefits

Remember the Six Magic Words in Sales

Somebody once told me the six most important words in sales…

What that means to you is…

Here's the difference between a feature and a benefit.

Features appeal to logic. A feature is a fact. **BENEFITS, ON THE OTHER HAND, APPEAL TO EMOTIONS**, and in general people make decisions based on emotions – how they feel about the product or service.

A feature tells us what it is. A benefit tells us what it will do for us.

Feature: *This game is designed with 64 bit CGI graphics and 256 color design. It is the result of the work of a team of 125 designers over three years. It is compatible with multiple game consoles.*

Benefit: *This game ROCKS. The graphics will blow you away. You gotta get this game dude!*

Feature: *This baby has a 210 Horsepower Engine*

Benefit: *What that means to you is when you're going uphill trying to merge on the highway you step on the gas and you're going to have plenty of power to merge safely. That's important, isn't it?*

Feature: *These tires are steel belted.*

Benefit: *What that means to you is they won't blow out on the highway and put you in a bad situation. Safety first, right?*

Feature: *This server has 18 slots for memory.*

Benefit: *What that means to you is that as your needs grow a few years down the road, you will be able to add more memory and extend the life of this server for a few more years, extending your investment. Makes sense, doesn't it?*

Feature: *This washing machine has a 3.4 cubic foot basin.*

Benefit: *That's important to you because you can throw your big bulky comforters in this washing machine with room to spare. Based on what you told me about the size of your family, this large basin is going to come in handy, isn't it?*

Feature: *This software comes with three years of support and is renewable year to year.*

Benefit: *What that means to you is that every time we update the software you will receive the update for free as part of your support contract. You're covered.*

Feature: *We have 24 hour phone support.*

Benefit: *That's important because at any time, for any reason you can call this number (then hand him the phone number) and you will be immediately connected to a live person – no recorded phone trees. You can dial the number right now and try it for yourself.*

Feature: *These cabinets are all cherry wood.*

Benefit: *That's really going to help you down the road with your resale value. Your house will be worth more money when you go to sell it.*

(notice you don't actually have to say the exact words: what that means to you is)

Every product or service is different, but you must find the emotional reasons to help your customers reach a decision.

Logic is great, but when you reach your customer's emotions – give them a personalized reason to buy - their level of interest in your product will soar.

Remember the six magic words that link the feature to the emotional benefit:

What that means to you is...

Add ENTHUSIASM to Your Pitch

No sale is made until there is a transfer of enthusiasm from the salesperson to the customer.

Explaining your product or service is great. You can describe its features, then relate each of those features to specific benefits that you know your customer will appreciate.

But we are going to focus now – not on what you say – but how you say it. I'm going to use CAPITAL LETTERS to indicate enthusiasm in my voice.

You've heard people say that in order to sell a product or service you must be passionate about it yourself. You must believe, beyond a shadow of a doubt, that this product or service is going to be the BEST THING for your customer. That BELIEF comes through with ENTHUSIASM.

Here are four steps in mastering sales.

1. A beginning salesperson still fumbles with product knowledge. They don't take the time to really dig in and understand the product or service at a detailed, deeper level.

2. An average salesperson is a product/service expert – and by the way, this is where most sales training is focused. They understand a lot about their product or service and are comfortable with the explanation / demonstration.

3. An advanced salesperson not only understands his product/service in great detail, but can explain the product features AND can explain how those features relate to the customer (Features / Benefits).

4. The MASTER SALESPERSON SELLS those benefits with ENTHUSIASM.

Here are examples of what this means in real situations.

Here's a terrible salesperson – no product knowledge.

"This car has a really great engine. People that know engines are saying it's the best on the market."

Here's a salesperson that knows his product.

"The Gizmo 3500 engine is 3.0 liters with more than 200 horse power and a five speed automatic transmission (features)."

Here's a good salesperson who adds the benefits of this engine.

"It gives you plenty of power, but also gets you up to 32 miles per gallon which will save you money at the pump (benefits)."

This is perfectly fine.

But here's a BETTER way to present that same engine – with ENTHUSIASM – which is going to make this engine far more attractive in the customer's mind. Here's a MASTER SALESPERSON.

"Are you familiar with the Gizmo 3500 engine? There is so much EXCITEMENT about this engine in the industry right now because it uses NEW COMPOSITE MATERIALS AND ADVANCED ENGINEERING TECHNIQUES to give you more than 200 horse power – which is going to give you a FEELING OF POWER LIKE A RACE CAR when you're merging onto the highway. But NOT ONLY is it one of the most powerful engines on the market, it's INCREDIBLY FUEL-EFFICIENT. You're going to get MORE THAN 32 MILES PER GALLON. You're going to save money at the gas pump EVERY SINGLE WEEK. By the end of the year you will have saved a TON OF MONEY on gas. People are SHOCKED to find out that an engine THIS POWERFUL will also get that great level of gas mileage. It's pretty much EVERYTHING YOU WANT IN AN ENGINE, isn't it?"

You have to listen to how you are presenting your product/service and take time to RE-WRITE YOUR SCRIPT so that you are not just listing the benefits, but TRULY SELLING the benefits. You have to be like an actor – don't just stand up there and read the script. You need to BECOME the part you are playing. BELIEF, PASSION, ENTHUSIASM. If you don't have it – you need to get it.

At that moment you are the only person standing between that customer and that product. You are the professional representative of your product or service and your company. If you don't have the passion for the product or service, how can your customer be passionate about it? How can your customer be attracted to it?

Without enthusiasm your customer leaves thinking *"Six of one, half a dozen of the other. I could go either way. It really doesn't matter."*

The enthusiasm in your presentation is what triggers the interest, the desire, the attraction in the customer's mind for your product or service. If there is no attraction or desire, there is no sale.

When you have created that attraction in the customer's mind, your closing skills fall right into place.

Here are a few more examples.

"We treat against EVERY type of household bug. It's unlikely, but if you EVER see a bug in your house, you now have ONE PHONE NUMBER TO CALL and within 24 HOURS GUARANTEED we will be there to take care of that problem – and that is NO EXTRA COST in addition to our normal quarterly service. We want our customers to NEVER HAVE TO WORRY ABOUT bugs in their house EVER AGAIN. How does that sound?"

"This publication is targeted to EXACTLY the type of people you need to be in front of. This is UNPARALLELED EXPOSURE for half

the price of other forms of advertising. But you even get MORE VALUE when you advertise with us because we feature you on our INDUSTRY LEADING WEBSITE visited by MORE THAN 10,000 INDUSTRY LEADERS EVERY WEEK. This program gives you the BEST BANG FOR YOUR BUCK, don't you think?"

"This software is TAKING OVER THE MARKET SO QUICKLY, but there are lots of good reasons why it's happening. We have targeted this solution to SMALL and MID SIZE BUSINESSES, so you don't get all the UNNECESSARY OVERHEAD of a Fortune 500 solution, and that allows us to enter the market AT THE PERFECT PRICE POINT. It's a MODULAR SOLUTION, so you start with ONLY WHAT YOU NEED at MINIMAL UP FRONT cost. And we have CONTINUED TO IMPROVE our support capabilities. We LISTENED VERY CAREFULLY to our customers and determined that 24 hour support was CRUCIAL to keeping our customer's operations running. The quality of our support is UNPARALLELED in the industry – so not only do we make is SO EASY to get started, but we also TAKE AWAY ALL THE WORRY after you've transitioned. You can see why this solution has been gaining in popularity so quickly, right?"

"The workmanship on these cabinets is the HIGHEST QUALITY you will find. You can spend THOUSANDS OF DOLLARS MORE and frankly, all you're getting for that money is the brand name. The workmanship from this company SURPASSES even the most well known high end brands. So you get the HIGHEST QUALITY AVAILABLE at MID-RANGE pricing. So WHY PAY SO MUCH MORE FOR A BRAND NAME if you're really not getting anything for it?

So here's your assignment. Listen to your presentation as you do it now. Make a long list of the BENEFITS (not the features) – you've got to know your benefits – luxury, power, capacity, economy, value, best, lowest, least expensive, best warranty, easy as 1, 2, 3, simple, precise, etc. Then write your benefits script with PASSION AND ENTHUSIASM pointing out and embellishing on every little benefit your product or service is going to bring to your customer.

Can you see how this one change will make an INCREDIBLE DIFFERENCE in your effectiveness?

Capturing Your Customer's FULL Attention

What if we could look into the minds of the very best salespeople and find the exact words and phrases they use to capture a customer's attention and interest - and then use those exact words and phrases ourselves?

I surveyed a small, select group of the most successful salespeople with the highest closing ratios, and I found three things they all have in common - one of those three things will completely surprise you, and I will share that with you at the end of my presentation.

The two sentences above are designed to capture your attention, to draw you towards me in anticipation. You're wondering: "What are the exact words and phrases that top salespeople use? What are the three things they all have in common? And particularly, what is the one that will surprise me?"

Public speakers use very specific strategies to immediately capture the attention of their listeners. Average speakers begin with the usual - *"hello I'm John Smith, Vice President of Sales at ABC Industries, and I am delighted to have the opportunity to speak with you today. ABC is the leading provider of.... blah blah blah."*

And you can give a perfectly good speech with a dry, boring opening - but great speakers immediately capture your attention and draw you in throughout their talk.

What if we could go into the mind of these great speakers and pull out their secrets?

Not only do they immediately capture your attention, THEY SET YOUR MIND TO A STATE OF WAITING EXPECTATION. They promise you something, and now you are going to listen intently for the payoff.

Before they even introduce themselves they say something like...

"I've always wondered what it would be like if..."
"Which approach do you think would work better..."

"We all face a very difficult choice..."

"How do the very best people in the world solve the problem of... have you ever wondered?"

"There are two skills you need that will lead to closing a lot more sales than you are now..."

"You have two choices..."

"Over the past four years our company has been brainstorming with a select group of our most successful clients, and we have come up with three game changing pieces of advice..."

"Do you remember the first time you..."

"What if we could look into the minds of the very best salespeople and find the exact words and phrases they use to capture a customer's attention and interest - and then use those exact words and phrases ourselves?"

And I also said... *"I surveyed a small, select group of the most successful salespeople with the highest closing ratios, and I found three things they all have in common - one of those three things will completely surprise you."*

The word "surprise" is one of the most attention grabbing words you can use. It sets their mind to a state of waiting expectation. They are listening for the surprise. If you start by asking a great question or promising great new information, your listeners will wait in anticipation of the payoff.

Obviously, if you're asked to say a few words or give a presentation - you want to use this type of introduction to immediately grab the attention of your audience.

But is there a way to use these same techniques in our own sales conversations?

Unfortunately, most people are poor listeners. So when you're talking to your customers, you can assume they are not good listeners, they are distracted, or they are anxious to interrupt you.

So choose your words and phrases, and your tone of voice to pull people in immediately.

> "We did some research, and were surprised at the results..."
> "We were shocked at what we found!"
> "This is a game changer..."
> "This solves a very important problem, and it solves it in a very unique way..."
> "We discovered three things that the best _____ do all the time, and we wanted to find out exactly how they do it."
> "You have two choices. Which one do you think would work better..."
> "What if we could..."
> "I was very surprised to find..."
> "What if we could look at this from a completely different angle..."

Try adding the subtle skill of opening your communications with a promise to deliver great new information. You will not only get their full attention, you will create in their minds a sense of waiting expectation. They will wait to hear what you have to say, and wait to hear how the story ends. Then, when you're ready you give them the payoff.

A Disarming Sales Approach

Because People Buy From People They Like

Many top salespeople have mastered a disarming style of communication. Rather than presenting and pushing the sales process along, these salespeople slow down, have a personal chat, develop a personal relationship, and simply agree with just about everything a customer says. It's a style that some people were born with, but it involves a series of techniques and approaches that any of us can learn and incorporate into our own style.

Even if the slow, casual, friendly style is not your style, you can still learn a lot from this approach, and add these ideas to your own sales skill set.

The most important lesson you can take from this approach is to SLOW DOWN. Most salespeople feel like they are imposing on the customer's time, so they rush through the presentation. When you catch yourself rushing, slow way down.

We are told that society has sped up so much in the past 25 years that nobody has the time to talk slowly any more, but that's not true. When the chemistry is right, you will be surprised, people are happy to settle in and have a friendly, productive conversation.

As you are talking you are not hiding the fact that you are a salesperson, you simply have the attitude:

I'm your buddy
This is just a pleasant chat
Us nice people need to stick together

Don't mistake this disarming style with being soft or afraid to close. These guys bring in huge customers, because the message in the customer's mind is *"This guy is different than other salespeople who call me. He is so easy to deal with, we're going to start moving our business to him."*

Because we are slowing the pace, there is plenty of opportunity for questions, listening and follow-up questions. There is plenty of opportunity to get your story in without feeling like you have to rush through it. There is plenty of opportunity to show yourself as an expert and a trusted advisor – no need to rush.

Slowing the pace and taking the time to listen creates a very positive feeling in your customer's mind.

This sales approach simply assumes that everyone you talk to is a nice person who enjoys talking to another nice person, and is going to give you all their business. They are not going to give you some of their business, they are going to give you ALL of their business.

These disarming salespeople say things like:

You don't have to...
Don't feel obligated... But if you do, it might be a good idea, you know?
I don't know if you want to take advantage of this... but it seems like a really good deal.

You don't have to decide now – you can do this any time. But did you see that...
I'm so glad you said that...
I'm so glad you asked that question...
Well you know, we do it this way – that's just us... you might be different.

*** That's a great question. You need to be completely comfortable with us because we will be doing a lot of business together for many years.

When an objection comes up...

"Exactly. I understand. That's why we..."

Agree, agree, agree.

I'm going to be out for a few days (no rush), but I'll be back Tuesday and we'll chat about this again and get this moving.

Because you're buddies, there's no doubt that he's going to take your call on Tuesday. If you end up leaving a voice message, he won't delete it. You will probably be the only sales message he doesn't delete – and he'll probably call you back.

Salespeople who have this disarming approach are never worried. They aren't worried about selling today. If they had some good conversations, they know they are going to get the full payoff down the road.

You've got to know your product and your industry cold. You've got to understand the sales process. You've got to have skills within skills within skills. You've got to be a master of words and phrases and influence. You've got to have all this, but in the end, **if you can relax, slow yourself down, and master this disarming sales approach, you're riding the wave of the most powerful principle in sales – people buy from people they like.**

Things Every Salesman Should Know

Impulsive Opposition

Impulsive opposition is a really simple idea that will help you open more conversations with customers.

Human beings are wired to disagree. We are wired to chime in with some interesting nugget, some additional information, add value, take the opposing side in an argument.

We do this unconsciously. If I walk into work and say "I hear it's going to be a beautiful weekend," someone will invariably say "I heard it might rain," or "I think it's going to be a hot one." Very seldom would someone answer, "Yes I also think it's going to be beautiful."

Psychologically we are wired to add value, so we typically say something which is opposite or different.

Here's how to use Impulsive Opposition to your advantage.

Look at these examples and come up with some more of your own. Listen carefully to how you word your questions, and then alter them slightly to generate a positive response.

Bad Question / "Oppositional" Response

"Can I help you?"
"No thanks. Just browsing."

"Is this a good time to talk?"
"Well actually, no it's not. I'm heading into a meeting."

"Is this within your budget?"
"No. That's much more than we can afford."

"What do you think about the price?"
"Well, that's more than we wanted to pay."

"Do you have any other projects we can help you with?"
"No. That's it for now. You've been great. Thanks."

"Do you need any accessories to go with that dress?"
"No. This will be all for now. Thank you so much."

"Would you like a Frequent Shoppers Card?"
"No thanks. That's ok."

Now let's look at these questions again and change them slightly to generate a more open and productive response.

Bad Question / "Oppositional" Response	Better Question / Open Response
"Can I help you?"	*"What are you shopping for?"*
"No thanks. Just browsing."	*"Well we wanted to look at...."* Or... *"Are you shopping for yourself or for a gift for someone else?"* Or... *"Do you know exactly what you're looking for?"* *"Yes we do."* Or *"No we don't."* Either way you can now help them.

"Is this a good time to talk?"	"Did I catch you at a bad time?"
"Well actually, no it's not. I'm heading into a meeting."	"No. I have a minute. What can I do for you?"
"Is this within your budget?"	"This won't break your budget will it?"
"No. That's much more than we can afford."	"No it won't."
"What do you think about the price?"	"That's not too much to pay for this solution, is it?"
"Well, that's more than we wanted to pay."	"No it's not."
"Do you have any other projects we can help you with?"	"What other projects are you planning?"
"No. That's it for now. You've been great. Thanks."	Or… "What else do you have going on?" Or… "That's not your only project, is it?" "Well, in a few weeks we will be ….."
"Do you need any accessories to go with that dress?"	"Have you seen our new handbags?"
"No. This will be all for now. Thank you so much."	"No I haven't."
"Would you like a Frequent Shoppers Card?"	"Have I shown you the Frequent Shoppers Program?"
"No. That's ok."	"No you haven't."

Making very small changes in your questions opens up more opportunities and pretty soon you will be making much more money.

Implicit Agreement / Tag Questions

This technique is the mirror image of Impulsive Disagreement. Here you are getting people to agree with you, to nod their head up and down – implying "yes what you say makes sense".

By wording your statements and including a simple Tag Question, people will almost always agree with you. It's implicit agreement because you are not asking them to answer, you're telling them – giving them a command - you're not really asking. You just want them to grunt or nod their agreement – asking for implicit agreement.

Here's how it works...

As you make statements, reinforce them with Tag Questions. Very simply, add a question after your statement. It's a simple and powerful way to reinforce your own statements. If they say "yes" then that's great – you're getting incremental agreement. If they say "no" or start to tell you why they don't agree then that's great too. They are giving you more information on exactly where you stand.

> "This looks like it will do the trick, doesn't it?"
> "It's time to brush your teeth, isn't it?" (if you're a salesman AND a parent)
> "This might be a better way to do it, don't you think?"
> "That's one feature you're not going to find anywhere else, you know?"
> "And it's such a time saver, isn't it?"

Doesn't it?
Wouldn't it?
Wouldn't you?
Don't you think?
You know?
Right?
Am I right?
Isn't it?
Won't it?

You can come up with hundreds of these statements as they apply to your situation.

Write them down. If you sell in person you can memorize them and look for opportunities to use them. If you sell on the phone you can keep the list in front of you. Make a small tick-mark each time you use one. Within a few days this will become a habit.

Specifically, tie these statements to the information you uncovered during your needs development process.

"Based on what you've told me, this is going to be a perfect fit, don't you think?"
"In your situation, this feature is going to be a real time saver, won't it?"
"This gives you such a sense of confidence, doesn't it?"
"That shirt has exactly the style you're looking for, doesn't it?"

Since you already know what's important to them, each key feature can be followed with a statement.

"That would save you a lot of money, wouldn't it?"
"That's a great feature, isn't it?"
"I bet that would make your job a lot easier, wouldn't it?"
"I bet that would attract more customers, wouldn't it?"
"That one feature pays for the whole system, doesn't it?"
"I bet your wife would appreciate that, wouldn't she?"

"I want to make sure we're getting you the right solution for your needs, you know?"
"This will be a good fit, right?"
"This will meet your needs better than the one we were looking at earlier, won't it?"
"You might be better off with a larger model, you know?"
"Your wife might appreciate the upgrade package, wouldn't she?"
"That's a good price, don't you think?"
"Being able to _____ is a real time saver, isn't it?"
"If you start off with Plan A, you can always upgrade to Plan B when you have the money, right?"
"These tires are much safer than the cheaper ones. Spending that extra money is worth it, don't you think?"
"You might as well get that radiator replaced now before you end up stuck on the highway somewhere, you know?"
"I have you down for two – you should probably get a spare in case one of these goes down at some point – that way you don't have to wait 24 hours to get back up and running, you know?"
"This is a great compromise, isn't it?"
"It makes sense to move on this while they are still available, doesn't it?"
"It's lucky we had that in stock, isn't it?"
"That's a fair solution, don't you think?" (everyone wants to be seen as fair)
"This seems like a reasonable way to handle it, doesn't it?" (everyone wants to be seen as reasonable)
"This is a reasonable compromise, isn't it?"

This is a very simple technique, and you should be able to find many places in your presentation and general conversation to insert an implicit agreement question, don't you think?

Green Light, Yellow Light, Red Light

Here are a few simple changes in wording that you can use – it's called Green Light, Yellow Light, Red Light.

The whole point of selling is to make it easier for the customer to buy.

The words you use and the way you phrase things make a very big difference in the perception other people have. This is particularly important when you are on the phone because the conversation can end abruptly and you may not have a chance to recover.

Instead of saying what you don't do and what you can't do – emphasize what you can do. Then redirect to a needs development question, or a closing statement.

Customer:	"Hello. I'm looking for part number 1234."
Red Light:	"I don't have any of those in stock."
Yellow Light:	"I don't have that exact part number."
Green Light:	"You've come to the right place. I have a shipment of that exact item arriving in 3 days."
Green Light:	Green light, then redirect to an upsell question.
	"I can have that in your hands by Friday. What else are you looking for?"

Green Light:	Green light, then redirect to a closing statement.
	"I have an identical / compatible part. Do you need this overnighted, or is Ground shipping ok?" (you told them what you can do, then redirected to a close)
Green Light:	Green light, then redirect to an open ended information gathering question.
	"I can have that in your hands by Friday. Is this the first time you're ordering from us? What kind of a project are you working on?" (green light, then redirect to an information gathering question – this could be a huge project if you find out more information)
Customer:	*"We were looking to stay under $500."*
Red Light:	*"Everything here starts at $1,000."*
Yellow Light:	*"That's going to be tough to do, but I'll try to make that happen."*
Green Light:	Ignore the problem and go directly into Needs Development
	"Fantastic. Tell me a little about what you had in mind."
	"Tell me a little more about what you were thinking."
	"Here's my commitment to you. I'm going to give you the best value possible – does that sound fair?"

These different statements have a very significant impact on the customer's thinking. In each of these responses you're telling the truth. But some of the answers immediately cut the conversation short, while others invite more information, and/or move you to a close.

Listen carefully to how you phrase things and how you respond to questions – you may find that even though you're being completely honest, you're pushing people away.

This is an area where you should listen to how other salespeople in your organization phrase things. You can actually hear them shut off a conversation with a red light response. Or you can 'borrow' green light phrasing from the other sales reps.

Even with a 'green light' response, you still may not be getting to the bigger picture, and you could be missing opportunities.

Green Light and a close to end the conversation:

"Yes I have that part. That will be $10. Which credit card are you using today?"
OK great. I'm going to use my Amex.

Try this instead.

Green Light and opening up to a deeper opportunity / relationship:

"Absolutely I have that part. What project are you working on? Is this the first time you've purchased from us? I'm so glad you found us. What else do you need?"

Well actually, I might need a million of this other item, but you probably don't carry that.

The Pattern Interrupt

My wife and I sit down at a restaurant looking forward to enjoying our meal and we are talking about our day, probably talking about our kids and what they are up to. Then the waitress comes and takes our drink order and asks us if we want any appetizers. After the waitress leaves I look back at my wife and say "What were we talking about?" She doesn't remember either.

We were thinking and talking about something, then the waitress interrupted our train of thought. Poof! It's gone.

Hypnotists and magicians use this technique to distract you from what you were thinking about and draw your attention to something new – something they want you to think about.

You can use this technique when the customer is not talkative, or not being cooperative, or the conversation is tracking in a negative direction – not going the way you would like.

On the phone creating a pattern interrupt is very easy.

> "I hear my name being paged - can you hold for one second? Thanks."
> "My wife is trying to reach me on my cell – can you hold for one second? Thanks."
> "Someone just walked up to my desk – can you hold for one second? Thanks."

After a few seconds you get back on the phone and you can start a brand new conversation about anything. You are free to completely change the topic of the call and create an entirely new chemistry.

"Did you see the end of the Cowboys game? Can you believe they ran the ball on 3rd down?"

"I never did ask you, what does your company do?"

"What were we talking about, you said something about a problem you were having."

"I never did ask you, did Bob leave the company or just take another position there?"

"I never did ask you, what were you doing before you took this position?"

"I just read an article about the government issuing a new regulation – what impact will that have on your company?"

You can ask a relationship question, a needs development question, tell a joke – anything to start fresh and create a positive tone to the conversation.

To use a pattern interrupt in person you need to either ask to use the rest room, or receive an imaginary text which is very serious and will require "just a second" of your time.

"I'm sorry. What were we talking about? How 'bout them Broncos!"

Implied Questions

If you can't ask questions, you shouldn't be in sales. As hard as I find it to believe, there are still salespeople who are not comfortable asking questions.

Here's a way to ask a question without actually asking a question. This is the least intrusive way to get people talking.

I use this opening when I'm cold calling on large opportunities, and I have finally reached the right person. I don't want to start the conversation with a series of questions because I feel they would be resistive, and I don't want to go on for five minutes about me and my product or service because I know they won't be listening.

I use one of the statements below, then pause and wait for them to start talking.

> "Hi Jack, this is Alan at XYZ Widgets. I just wanted to talk to you and find out a little about what you do, make sure you know about what we do, and how we might be able to do some business together."

I just made a statement. I never asked a question, but if I just pause after the statement, it's perceived as a question.

95 out of 100 people will start telling you about what they do and what they are looking for.

> "I just wanted to talk to you for a second..."

> "I was hoping you could explain / bring me up to date / help me understand / fill me in ..."
> "I just wanted to find out about..."

Here are some other examples of gathering information without actually asking a question.

> "If I knew more about the full extent of your project, I would be able to narrow down the focus."

> "I was wondering who else is going to be part of this decision."
> "I was wondering who else will need to see this presentation."
> "I was wondering who else we will need to convince to get this rolling."
> "If I knew more about your business, we could quickly determine if we are a good fit or not."
> "I was wondering what your asking price is."
> "I'm just calling to find out what air conditioning equipment you have installed."
> "I was wondering who your current vendor is."
> "I was wondering if you have a budget in mind for this project."

The Embarrassed Questions

Most good salespeople can say anything to anybody – they have no fear. But even the best salesman gets uncomfortable when asking some sensitive questions.

Sometimes you need to ask a sensitive question but you may be a little shy or uncomfortable asking. Start the question by almost apologizing.

I hate to ask...

I probably shouldn't ask...

I hesitate to bring this up, but...

Imagine if you were an Undertaker?

"I hate to ask, but how will you be paying for this?"

He doesn't have any easy questions.

Future Tense

Imagine What it Will Be Like

"Picture yourself on a boat on a river"

—*The Beatles*

Future tense is a very effective suggestive technique that puts your customer's mind to work imagining themselves enjoying the benefits of your product or service. It helps them feel comfortable moving forward because they have already pictured themselves after the transaction.

It's not a trick. It actually helps people picture your benefits. You know how great people feel after they have made the decision to move forward. This helps people picture all those great feelings right now.

> *Imagine after installing this software, you will have a single interface to manage all your equipment.*
>
> *What are some of the things you're planning to do after you sell your company?*
>
> *When this remodeling project is complete and you walk into this room, you will have the full view of the sunset - imagine how different that will feel than the view you have now.*
>
> *Based on what you told me, this system will save you about $800,000 per year. Imagine what you will be able to accomplish with that extra cash flow.*
>
> *After you have ordered from us two or three times you will get a real sense of the importance of working with a*

company that stands behind their products, answers the phones, and really goes all out to support its customers. Imagine calling in with a problem and talking to real person instead of hearing a recording "press 1 for accounting" "press 2 for a company directory".

As soon as you give me the go-ahead we will schedule a detailed review of your past three years tax returns to look for some immediate savings.

Imagine coming home from work and walking up these stairs to this view of the backyard and see your children playing back there.

Picture your ad right there on that web page where thousands of targeted customers will see your brand name every day.

Imagine pulling into your driveway an hour from now and honking your horn and your children come running out onto the driveway to see this car. Then go take them all out for some ice cream in the new car!

After you join this health club, imagine how good you will feel in just a few weeks. In fact, I'm going to make a note in my calendar for three weeks from now, and if you don't see me I want you to come into my office. I want to hear how much better you feel.

Of the five houses we visited today, which one can you picture yourself living in right now?

Reflecting and Paraphrasing

When your customer is talking you want him to continue to talk. You want him to give you more information because this makes it easier for you to match your product or service to what the customer has already told you he needs.

A good listener is like a green light, inviting the speaker to continue.

Reflecting is the easiest listening technique, and it is the ultimate green light to the speaker.

You reflect (or mirror) the exact words or phrases back to the speaker, but inflect your voice to denote a question. (Husbands, if you do this with your wives they will think that you are really listening to them! It works every time!)

When you reflect, people just keep telling you more and more. You're not really saying anything, but people feel like you are listening to them (which you are!).

Listening in general, and reflecting in particular is an opportunity to learn more, gain credibility, open up new needs and deeper areas of questioning, deepen your relationship, become a trusted advisor, sell more, make more money.

"We've had some quality problems lately that have cost us a lot of money."

"Quality problems?"

Reflecting is a "green light" that gives the speaker a chance to tell you more.

Here are some "yellow light / red light" responses that tend to stop the conversation, or even create the negative feeling that you're not listening.

"Well you won't have any quality problems with our solution."

"I wouldn't expect your company to have quality problems."

"I can't believe you had quality problems. What did you pay for that system?"

"I had another customer tell me the same thing yesterday."

The above examples are not really listening. You heard what your customer said, then you interjected your own stories and opinions. You are talking, not listening.

More examples of reflecting:

"I'm looking for a very low cost solution."
"Very low cost?"

"They are having some problems with the new rollout."
"Problems?"

"Where are you from?"
"Cleveland."
"Cleveland?"

How was your day honey?
Hectic.
Hectic?

Reflecting is the easiest technique to use, but we all have a strong urge to inject our own comments, or change the subject, or judge the other person's statement. Whenever you ask a question, make an effort to simply reflect. This not only allows you to gather more information, it is respectful of the other person and they will feel good about you.

This is the single most important relationship building tool.

Paraphrasing is very similar to reflecting, and is another easy, but effective listening technique. Paraphrasing gives the speaker a green light to tell you more.

To paraphrase, simply take what they said to you, and repeat it back to them in your own words. You can also end the sentence with a question inflection.

"We're having some problems with the new rollout."

Reflecting: *"Problems?"* or *"Problems with the rollout?"*

Paraphrasing: *"So the new rollout hasn't been very smooth?"*

Either way, reflecting or paraphrasing, they will give you more information.

"How was your day honey?"

Hectic.

Hectic? Reflecting

Wow so you had a crazy day? Paraphrasing

"The new factory is coming online in April and should help with the overflow."

"So you are using the new factory for overflow?"

Or *"It's coming on line that soon?"*

These paraphrasing statements are very helpful in getting your client to tell you more.

"So what you're saying is..."

"Are you saying...?"

"I want to make sure I've understood you correctly."

"This is important. Let me make sure I've got it right..."

"You said something earlier that caught my attention, and I want to make sure I understand..."

Here's a quick story about paraphrasing.

There was a new young saleswoman who was starting with the company and they had her sit with me for a day to listen in on my calls. I was going to conference her in, then she was going to put her phone on mute, so she could listen to both sides of the conversation. Well for some reason her phone was not working right, and we were not able to conference her in, so I had her roll her chair over to me so she could at least hear my side of the conversation – even though she couldn't hear the customer.

When I got through to a customer, she could only hear me, so I repeated everything the customer said so she could know what the customer said, and then she could hear my response.

When I got off the phone I said to myself – "wow I'm the king of paraphrasing – that was awesome." In fact, I had paraphrased for the benefit of this new sales trainee who couldn't hear what the customer was saying.

So now when I want to work on paraphrasing I pretend there is someone sitting next to me trying to listen to the whole conversation, but can only hear my side – so I have to repeat what the customer is saying.

It really works.

Try to improve your listening skills on every call from now on by practicing Reflecting and Paraphrasing.

Question Technique

Probe and Clarify

The single skill that differentiates the above average sales professionals from the average is their ability to ask questions.

Questions allow you to pull more information from the speaker.

One of the very first jobs I ever had was as a telephone survey taker. I was one of those people who would call you in the middle of dinner. I hated the job, but I learned how to ask questions like a pro.

I got paid $5.50/hour plus a $5 bonus for every "3 x 3" survey I turned in (and that was back in the day when $5 meant something!). As an example, suppose we were doing a survey of people who had recently taken a business skills workshop. In order to complete the "3 x 3" survey and get paid the $5 bonus, I had to get three things they liked about the workshop, with three specific examples of each, and then three things they didn't like about the course.

Probe: What did you like about this seminar?

"It's useful on my job."

Clarify: What do you mean by useful?

"I can apply it immediately to real situations when I get back to work."

Paraphrase: Oh so you can apply it to real situations when you get back to work. (paraphrase)

"Exactly."

Probe: What else about the class did you find useful? (open ended question)

"It covered some topics that I will use at work."

Clarify: Oh what were some of those topics that were the most useful?

Etc.

What else did you like about this course?

"The instructor was good."

Great you had a good instructor. What did you like about the instructor?

"Well, he seems to have really thought about listening more than most people."

So you would say he was an expert listener? (paraphrase)

"Yes definitely."

What else did you like about the instructor?

"He really handled questions very well."

Oh he was good with questions?

What else about the instructor did you like?

"He stayed on topic and got us out on time each day."

What were some other things you liked about the course?

Etc. etc. etc.

When my 3 x 3 matrix was filled up and I wanted to get on to the next topic I would stop asking open ended questions (what, what else, why) and started asking closed ended questions.

Is there anything else you liked about the class? (almost always get an impulsive disagreement: "No that's about it").

Now what didn't you like about the course?

etc., etc., etc.

Then I would fill up three reasons with three specific examples on what they didn't like. Then I would pick up my $5 for the completed survey!

Like 1	Like 2	Like 3	Dislike 1	Dislike 2	Dislike 3
Useful	Instructor	Facility	Handouts	Duration	Too many students
Applied directly to my job	Expert listener	Good directions	Had mistakes	Didn't need to be 3 days	Not personal enough
Listening skill is very helpful	Handled questions well	Close to home	Bad quality copies	Started too early	Too many questions from too many people
How to ask questions	Stayed on topic	Nice room	Loose papers – needed to be in a notebook	Too many breaks	Not enough chairs
	Good time management	Good snacks			

Probe and clarify to gather more information. This is a really important skill because the more information you have, the better you will be able to match your solution to their needs.

These Listening skills and Questioning skills are critical to your success as a salesperson.

Imagine you are trying to break into a new account who is already using your competitor. If that competitor's salesperson is doing a good job asking questions, listening and understanding this customer – it is highly unlikely that you will be able to pull business away – because that salesperson is giving this customer what they need. On the other hand, if that salesperson has not taken the time to listen and understand, then by asking great questions, listening and understanding – you have a great shot at pulling the business away from your competitor.

You have to realize that every day there are salespeople calling on your best customers, and if you aren't asking, listening and understanding – those salespeople will pull your customers away every time.

Call your best customers today and ask, listen and understand. Then offer them creative ideas and services to better meet their needs. That's how you keep your customers.

Improve the Quality of Your Questions

It's not enough to ask questions, you need to constantly be on the lookout for better questions that get you more information.

Here are some standard questions:

"Who is the decision maker?"

"What's your timeline on this project?" / "When do you think you will get final approval?"

"Did you receive the quote I sent you?"

Great! You're asking questions. You are way ahead of half the salespeople in the world.

Now let's think about raising the quality of your questions. It's good to ask questions, but when you raise the level of your questions you will be able to get far more information from your customers – and open up opportunities for new questions.

Good Question	Better Question
"Who is the decision maker?"	"Can you walk me through your decision process?"
"What's your timeline on this?"	"Can you walk me through your timeline?"

"Did you receive the quote I sent you?"	"What did you think about the quote I sent you?" "Is it a bad time to review the quote I sent you?" "What's the next step on that quote I sent you?"
"Do you have any other projects coming up?"	"What other projects are you working on?"
"What other projects are you working on?"	"What are your plans for the next few months / years?"
"Who is your current vendor?"	"What are the factors you look for in a vendor?" "How can we get some of your business?"
"Is quality important to you?"	"How important is quality?" "What other factors are important?"

Exploratory Questions

The "Key and Pivot" Technique

We've talked about Needs Development questions. These will help you assess your customer's situation, and allow you to highlight the key elements of your product or service which best meet your customer's needs, and will be most important given his circumstances. Rather than just blathering on with your pitch - if you take a little time to understand your customer's circumstances - you can tailor your pitch to their specific needs. By asking assessment questions / Needs Development questions, you can build value by showing how your product or service meets his actual needs.

Exploratory Questions allow you to dig deeper into your customer's situation. To not only learn more about their situation, but to become more valuable to them. You'll see what I mean in a minute.

While many salespeople don't even ask questions - they simply rush into their presentation, most salespeople are taught to ask Needs Development questions, and most salespeople - if you listen to a few of their sales conversations - ask two or three of the same questions before they begin their presentation. And that's good. That's better than simply jumping into the pitch without knowing anything about the customer.

Other salespeople have a list of questions that they want to ask. As I will show you shortly, Exploratory Questions differentiate you from every other salesperson.

Exploratory Questions are an advanced sales technique. I call them advanced because they are not something you can list and memorize - asking Exploratory Questions involves an ability to respond - in real time - to your customer's comments and statements.

Key and Pivot

As your customer is talking listen for a key word in their sentence, then pivot on that key word to build an exploratory question. For example,

> *We have had problems in the past...*
> *"Tell me about some of the problems you have had."*
> *We are considering a few different options...*
> *"What are some of those options?"*
> *"What are the important elements that you are considering in each solution?"*
> *"What is the dominant factor that you are considering in your evaluation?"*
> *"Tell me a little about your evaluation process."*
>
> *We are happy with...*
> *"What is it you like about...?"*
> *"If you could change some things about... what would it be?"*
> *We are concerned about taking on a new...*
> *"Tell me more about what concerns you."*
> *"When you say 'concerned' tell me what that means."*
>
> *"You know, you said something earlier about.... Tell me more about that."*

A beginning salesperson is rushing to get into the presentation (because how can anyone buy my product/service if I don't explain it to them?), and when they do ask questions they interrupt the customer's answers.

But as an advanced salesperson, you are not wrapped up in your pitch - in fact, the sales process has very little to do with the pitch. You are hearing their statements, questions, objections and pivoting directly off their own statements - digging, exploring for more information, concerns, wants, needs, etc.

So Exploratory Questions are a two-step approach.

You hear certain words that come up:

Happy / Unhappy
Concerned / Nervous / Worried
Comfortable / Uncomfortable
Like / Don't Like
Issue / Problem
Opportunity
Solution
Satisfied / Unsatisfied
Affordable / Can't Afford
Schedule
Keeping / Changing
Optimum / Ideal
Less than ideal
Current vendor
Status Quo
Upset
Over burdened
Over budget
Budget conscious
Etc.

As you hear these key words, simply pivot on those words using Exploratory Questions to dig deeper.

"Tell me more about _____"
"Can you share more detail about _____"
"That's interesting. Can you give me a few examples"

"Help me understand"
"When you say ____, what does that mean?"
"What do you mean by _____?"
"What"
"Why"
"How"
"You said something earlier that was very interesting..."

Value Questions

The highest level of exploratory questions goes deeper into value, including personal value:

"How does this affect you?"
"What are you most worried about?"
"What are your priorities in a ...?"
"What do you value most in a ...?"
"Who else is impacted by your decision?"
"What are the implications of your decision?"
"How do you measure the cost of this problem?"
"What will this solution save you over time?"
"Why is this decision so important?"
"What's at stake here?"
"What impact does this decision have on the overall business?"
Why are exploratory questions effective?

It seems counter-intuitive. The customer is talking more than you are. You've hardly said anything, you just kept asking more and more questions. But when you go deep with Exploratory Questions - you are making a very powerful statement to your customer's UNCONSCIOUS MIND. What they hear (even though you haven't said a word about your solution) is that you are intelligent, competent, credible, honest, trustworthy. You are the one. And the truth is, they will never meet another person who will take the time to dig deeply into their situation.

The Final Pivot to a Partnership or Solution

By asking Exploratory Questions you are building trust and credibility, but how do you take advantage of this and move toward the next step – because eventually you have to propose a solution and close the sale?

The final step after exploratory questions is to pivot to a solution through partnership:

> "You have shared a lot of information with me – I appreciate that."
>
> "A lot of what you are experiencing is similar to what some of our other clients have experienced."
> "I would like to work with you on this."
> "Based on what you've told me, I'm confident we can help."
> "We are going to be able to develop a solution that will meet your needs."
>
> "How can we work together to make sure...?"
> "How can I help?"
> "What specifically does our solution need to address?"
> "How do we position...?"
> "Help me craft a proposal which will..."

Use the "Key and Pivot" Technique to rise above all other salespeople – become an expert listener, question asker, and explorer.

Moving Past the Putoff

"Send me some information about your company."

"I'll let you know if we're interested."

Great. I will put something together. What types of things are going to be most important for you to know? Assuming the information is good, walk me through what the next steps will be. After I send you the information, what date can we schedule to review your needs?

"Send me a quote and I'll forward it to the people who need to see it."

Great. I appreciate your commitment to do that. Can you give me some background about your priorities so I can make sure the quote addresses all your needs? The other people who are reviewing this proposal – what are the issues that are most important to them?

(If you know this person is just stonewalling, then one tactic is to ask a series of technical questions that they won't be able to answer. "I just want to ask a few questions so I can quote the right items – do you have 220V or 110V system? Do you know if you already have Version 3.3 installed?" Then "I think we need to get these other folks directly involved, you know?")

"All those decisions are made in Purchasing."

This is a real putoff. Usually you are talking to the right person or group – but now they are telling you to contact Purchasing - but purchasing will tell you they only buy what this group recommends.

"I will definitely work with your Purchasing group to register our company as a vendor, but Purchasing normally just buys what you recommend, don't they? What projects are you working on now that we could help you with?"

You may just have an uncooperative contact and you need to talk to someone who will be more willing to cooperate: "Can you walk me through your decision process, and exactly who specifies the equipment? At what point does the purchasing group get involved? Who is the primary decision maker for this type of project?"

"You need to talk to John."

Great. So I can get myself prepared, what do you think will be most important to John?

Can you walk me through your internal process and where everybody fits in?

"Call me back."

Sure. When would be the best time to call so you have a few minutes to talk? So I'm prepared, what will be the most important things you will want to discuss? What are your most pressing needs right now?

Getting the Appointment

Getting in to Meet With Them

Here's the scenario. You have just taken a job with a new company to manage your territory. Your territory might be the state, it might be the city, or it might be two or three counties.

You've got thousands of potential clients in your territory, and certainly hundreds of qualified customers in your territory.

Now you need to go meet them. LinkedIn, Networking events, Business Memberships – all great. But at some point you are going to have to get on the phone and start calling.

So how do you set the appointment?

Your goal is to target potential companies, get invited, then have your key contact come meet you in the reception area and invite you back into his/her office.

Later in the book, the Cold Calling section will get into a lot more detail on gatekeepers, voicemail and crafting an opening statement, but let's talk here specifically about setting an appointment.

Begin With the End Result – You Already Have the Appointment

To understand how to be successful at setting appointments, let's begin with the end result. In this case, let's suppose you have successfully set an appointment. You have been invited to visit the company and you have been given 15 minutes, maybe 30 minutes, or maybe an hour to meet with a key contact.

If you have succeeded in gaining an appointment, it means...

- They are interested in you and your company
- They believe spending time with you is more valuable than whatever other activity they could be engaged in
- They believe you care about their business or situation
- They trust you
- They have confidence that you / your company is capable of positively impacting their business

The truth is, you weren't GIVEN the meeting, you EARNED the meeting.

So how do we EARN these meetings?

If you work for the biggest name in your industry – it's easy to get an appointment. Why is it so easy? Because they already trust you. They already know that you are credible. They already know you have solutions that other businesses use. With name recognition comes trust, confidence and credibility.

The sales rep from the big name company can call a target customer in the morning and get a lunch appointment at noon.

If you are the big company, if you have the top marketing brand, use your advantage to get appointments.

But the market is constantly changing. New companies are always challenging the big names, and creating their own reputations.

How do these no-name companies get in the door?

The only way you can get in the door is to gain trust, be seen as credible (both you and your company) and have something to offer which is perceived as valuable, different, or unique.

Before making the first phone call, ask yourself these questions:

Why would this person I'm about to call...

- Be interested in you and your company?
- Believe you add value, and that time spent with you is going to be worth it?
- Believe you care about their business or situation?
- Trust you?
- Believe that you / your company is capable of positively impacting their business?

If you can't answer these questions, then it will be very difficult to earn an appointment.

Now craft your entire first phone call toward answering these questions.

Why Do Your Customers Buy From YOU?

Every company must identify its value proposition. Your customers have other choices, so why do they work with you?

Is it the company?
Is it the product?
Is it your company's unique approach?
Is it the results you have already gotten with other customers?
Is it location?
Is it availability?
Is it the warranty?
Is it the support?
Is it the price?
Is it quality?
Is it service?
Is it you as the salesperson?

What have your customers gained by working with you / your company?

Why do they keep buying from you?

What is it that you offer to them that they can't get anywhere else?

As we will discuss in the Cold Calling section, you will spend time working your way through several different company contacts to identify the right person, but when you are talking to the right person, say something like this.

The goal is to make them WANT to meet with you.

The time they spend with you will be valuable for them.

You and your company are trustworthy and credible.

Your product and company have something of value to offer to them.

You and your company understand their business.

> *"Hello Mr. Customer, my name is Alan Gordon of ABC Bidgets Company. We take a very unique approach to Bidgets, and our unique approach has helped hundreds of companies save ____% on their Bidget budget. I think we might be able to do the same for you, and I wanted to meet with you briefly to determine if we might be a good fit. After a few minutes if we are not a good fit I'll tell you, and if we are a good fit, I'll tell you too. Does that sound reasonable?"*

One of three things will happen at this point.

- Resistance to being cold called, and they will use Control Statements
- They will present objections
- They will ask questions – which is a positive sign of interest

Here are some typical resistance / control statements which occur early in a Cold Call. The section on Cold Call Resistance and Control Statements will explain how to deal with these.

"Who are you again?"
"What is this about?"
"How did you get my number?"
"Take me off your list."
"I'm busy right now."
"Are you a salesman?"

Here are the some of the more common objections you will run up against.

"We already have a bidget vendor. So I'm really not interested in meeting with another vendor."
"Now is not a good time. We're fighting a hundred fires."
"Our CEO has put a freeze on spending, so any new project would be out of the question."
"Why can't we just do this on the phone?"

You need a prepared response to each of these objections. See the section on Handling Objections to help you craft a response to each one.

Then review the section on PRACTICING these objections so your responses are automatic.

Now if they ask questions like these, it is a positive sign of interest:

"I've never heard of your company."
"What company did you say you were with?"
"What other companies in my industry have you worked with?"
"Why do you think your approach is unique?"
"I'm pretty happy with my Bidget vendor, why would I want to work with you?"

These types of questions offer you the opportunity to engage in a dialog, and allow you to immediately go to your Needs Development questions.

If they want to engage further on the phone, by all means keep it going.

> *"How many bidgets do you normally order at a time?"*
> *"What size bidgets have you standardized on?"*
> *"When is your next order of bidgets coming up?"*
> *"How can I get that next order?"*
> *"I'm sending you our credit application for Net 30 payment terms. Go ahead and fill that out and I'll swing by to pick it up this afternoon."*

However, typically they will not give you the order on a first cold call. You will have to meet with them to build trust and credibility.

> *"You know Jack, a lot of the information you have shared with me on this call is going to be very helpful to me in preparing for our meeting. How is your calendar on Thursday?"*
> Why can't we just do this over the phone?
> *"I understand, you're concerned that an in person meeting might turn out to be a waste of your time. I can assure you, I'm not interested in wasting your time or mine. We will know very quickly how strong a fit we have. How is your calendar on Thursday?"*

So remember what you're selling:

The goal is to make them WANT to meet with you.

The time they spend with you will be valuable for them.

You and your company are trustworthy and credible.

Your product and company have something of value to offer to them.

You and your company understand their business.

When beginning a relationship, you're not focused on your product/service/solution. You are building trust and credibility by asking questions and understanding their business.

A Few More Tips About Appointments

Set the appointment as soon as possible to reduce the likelihood of a reschedule or cancellation.

Confirm the appointment via email the day before, and by phone AFTER or BEFORE business hours, again to reduce the likelihood of a reschedule or cancellation.

Get Them Physically Involved

If you've got a product that is three dimensional, use this technique all day.

> Feel how that door shuts. Listen to this other one. That's why this one is more expensive – it's built with sturdier materials so there will be less vibration, and that means the motor will last longer.

> Put your hand in there – see how much space you have?

> Here are the keys. Let's see if this car is as good as I've been saying it is.

> Here's our 24 hour tech support hotline. Dial the number right now. You will never have to wait more than 45 seconds to speak to a live certified technician.

> Feel the fibers on these two different carpets. Now you understand why one is $5.99 per square foot and the other one is $14.99 per square foot.

> Feel the quality of this wood vs. that wood?

> See how easy that is? Here, try it yourself.

Even if your product is not three dimensional – try to find ways to get your customer physically involved.

If you're demonstrating a product, let the customer do it rather than have him watch you the whole time.

Getting people physically involved gets them psychologically committed.

Tie the "New" to the "Old"

Habit Theory

Do you sell something "new" and "exciting".

> *"This product/service is a game changer. It's going to change the way you think about _____."*

Having something new and different is great. It's going to save your customers lots of time and money. It's all good.

Yet customers still hesitate and resist moving forward. Why would anyone want to stay with old, inefficient and more expensive when there's a much better solution at a lower cost?

One of the main reasons people don't move forward in sales is a fear of making a decision, fear of making a mistake, fear of doing something new.

During your presentation you take steps to show the customer how your product/service will save them time and money, or lead to increased revenues. Then you demonstrate that it's true – demonstrate physically, or with stories, or with a series of leading questions.

So once you have established that your product/service will save them time and/or money – why would any rational person not immediately move forward?

To overcome this fear of moving forward, let's explore one of the most interesting fields of psychological study: **Habit Theory**.

Research says that a full 60% of our daily activity is habit driven. Habits are important because they allow our minds to focus on the more important things and leave the mundane, repeating tasks to habit.

Our morning routines are entirely unconscious habit. I put on my left sock, then my right sock, then my left shoe, then my right shoe. Try changing the sequence and immediately something doesn't feel right.

We've all had the experience of "knowing" that we are forgetting something – we can't figure out what it is but we "KNOW" we are forgetting something. Sure enough, a few minutes later we remember what it is. If you feel like you're forgetting something, it's a very good bet that you probably are forgetting something.

Our morning commute is done almost completely unconsciously – by habit. 70% of automobile accidents happen within 10 miles of home. It's safe to say that the vast majority of these accidents happen during the commute to or from work. Accidents are much more likely to happen when you break your routine. For example, if one morning you have to stop by the bank on your way to work, you are off your routine and things just don't feel right.

Now let's circle back to the idea that customers have a fear of making a decision, or making a mistake, or doing something new.

Habit Theory explains why people hesitate to move forward with a great new product or solution – even though it is clear it will be to their benefit.

When it comes to customer psychology, the main reason people hesitate is because they are comfortable in their existing habits. They are uncomfortable even thinking about doing something new. Even if it is more expensive or more time consuming to do it the old way, they prefer doing it the old way. Habits are deeply ingrained in their unconscious mind.

They will give you all kinds of reasons for not moving forward - price, timing, need to think about it, etc. But in many cases the real reason is an unconscious psychological discomfort with habit change.

The more you remind them how new and exciting it is, the deeper their unconscious resistance to changing their current habits.

So we counteract this tendency during our presentation by tying our "new" product or service to their "old" way of doing things.

During your presentation, find comparisons and analogies that tie the new way of doing things to something they are familiar with.

> "It's as easy as brushing your teeth - you just take this one pill every morning then forget all about it"

> "You will use this system exactly the way you do now. In fact, all the user names and passwords will be exactly the same"

> "This is just like going to your doctor once a year for your checkup"

Rather than creating a whole new way of thinking, tie it to something they already do, or tie it to a habit they already have - it will greatly reduce their unconscious resistance. They will see your product or solution as the "same", not something "different" and unconsciously, they will be more receptive to moving forward.

References and Validation

You are paid to speak glowingly of your product and your company. That's your job. But to hear someone else describe their experience has far more value to a potential customer.

Remember, from the customer's perspective they may want to buy what you're offering, but they are unsure because they have to go through a psychological process before they will be able to feel comfortable with you. Your job is to guide them through this process, making it easier for them every step of the way.

References and testimonials are more effective if your customer can identify with them, whether they are down the street, or in the same industry. Gather and tailor your references and testimonials to match as closely as possible with your potential customer.

Validation is a slightly different concept. Validation means that you can prove to the customer that your product or service will do what you say it will.

If you have a letter from the government or a graph or a photo of the results – and they are guaranteed – that is validation.

All my clients are getting 20% returns.

Yeah right.

Here are the numbers going back 48 months.

Oh wow.

Most products and services are validated with stories. We had a client – pretty much in the same situation as you're in right now – who was very hesitant to commit to this. In fact, they took more than six months to sign a contract. Within four weeks they had etc. etc. etc.

Many objections result because people just don't believe that the benefits you're describing are actually going to happen for them in their specific circumstance. Anticipate this by focusing on validation early in the process to grow your credibility in the customer's mind.

The 45 Second Rule

LISTEN MORE. TALK LESS.

When you find yourself talking for more than 45 seconds – stop and ask a question. The easiest way to do this is to tell you how great my product is – talk, talk, talk - (now my internal clock says that I'm talking too much) and then just ask "Does that make sense?" or "What do you think?" or "How does that stack up against _____?" or "Have you heard that before?" or "Let me ask you a question."

But enough about me – let's spend our time talking about you!

In general, I don't want to be talking. When a call goes well I'm asking lots of questions and listening far more than I'm talking. When my 45 second clock times out, I stop and ask a question.

This idea of stopping yourself from talking too much – the 45 Second Rule - leads us directly into the concept of a trial close.

The Trial Close

Find Out Where You Stand

What is a Trial Close? You hear this phrase all the time, but in reality it's a very simple concept. You should naturally be doing this throughout the sales process.

A trial close lets you know where you stand, and identifies a customer's objections.

A Trial Close is nothing more than pausing and asking the following type of question.

> *How does this sound so far?*
> *What questions do you have?*
> *What do you think?*
> *What are your thoughts so far?*
> *How does this relate to your needs?*
> *From a value point of view, what do you think?*
> *How comfortable are you with what we have discussed so far?*
> *I know you said you were concerned about ___. Other than that, what other questions or concerns do you have?*
> *Does this make sense?*
> *Given your timeframe (situation/bosses opinion/past experiences/etc.) how does this sound?*
> *Obviously there are a few more details, but in general how does this sound to you?*
> *On a scale of one to ten – what do you think about this? Ok a 7? What are your concerns, and how can we turn that into a 10?*
> *Do you like it? Why? Why not?*

These Trial Close questions get one of four results:

1. They will be strongly interested
2. They will ask questions, asking for more information
3. They will state a concern (I'd like to do this, but I'm concerned about...)
4. They will pose an objection (I can't do this because...)

If they respond with strong interest you can move to a closing dialog by focusing on these types of things:

"Let's talk about getting this scheduled."

"Ok, let's give this a try and see how it works for you."

"Let's review to make sure we have covered everything that's important to you."

"There are still a few things we need to nail down before we start."

"Is there anything we haven't covered so far?"

"Ok great. The next thing I wanted to cover is..."

"We talked about A and B – which one would you prefer?"

"Normally we break the payments into two – I will write up the paperwork for the first payment right now."

"Where are we shipping this to?" or "Are we shipping this to the same address you wrote down earlier?"

Etc.

If they ask questions to gather more information, this is also a buying signal. They are interested, they are leaning forward (psychologically) and want more information. Answer their questions, then find out what other questions they have:

"That was a great question – I'm glad you asked that.
Does that clarify...?

Have we cleared that up?
Does that make you more comfortable?
Does that make you feel better about…?
What other questions do you have?" or *"what else do we need to cover?"*

Then move to a close with a tie-down. [Questions with a Tie-Down](#)

If, on the other hand, they respond with a concern, or a hesitation, or an objection – this next step is critical.

Uncover their concerns or objections:

"I can see that you're a bit hesitant. What are you concerned about?"
"I can sense a little hesitation or doubt. What are you concerned with?"
"Can you share some of your concerns?"
"What is your most important hesitation?"
"Tell me more about that."

These questions are critical.

You've talked, talked, talked. You've stopped and asked them "How does that sound?"

If interested – proceed toward a close, as appropriate.

If they ask a question – answer the question, get more questions, then proceed toward a close, as appropriate.

If hesitant – find out what they are concerned about. Explore their concerns, listen, and uncover more details about their concerns.

Many of their questions and concerns are resolved by just giving them more information – so if this is the case, you simply proceed with your presentation.

Objections are more serious, and simply continuing with the presentation will lose them. You have to dig deeper into their concerns by asking questions.

Whatever their response to your Trial Close questions, the Trial Close is an essential step to see where you stand.

Read more in the next chapter: Handling Objections – The Right Way.

Handling Objections

Here's the Right Way to Do it

As the sales process proceeds, your customers will go through a variety of psychological responses.

Sometimes the customer will be psychologically leaning towards you. They are interested. They trust you. They can picture themselves making this purchase. Other times they are psychologically leaning away from you. They don't believe this is for them. They don't like you. They don't believe you. They have doubts and concerns.

At the very beginning of this book we talked about how a professional fisherman understands how the fish behave. This is how your customers behave.

Questions Are Different Than Objections

When they are interested they lean in – asking questions is an indicator of interest, a buying signal. When you sense their interest, you move in for the close (either slowly or quickly depending on your type of sale) because it's a buying signal. This is called Questions with a Tie-Down.

When they are unsure or uncomfortable they lean away – concerns and objections are an indicator of discomfort or uncertainty.

Questions are asking for more information and are in most cases a BUYING SIGNAL, or at least a sign of interest.

In the previous section, we defined concerns as some circumstance which is standing in the way of moving forward. They are interested, BUT...

Objections, on the other hand, represent obstacles or uncertainties in the customer's mind.

Questions mean they want to know more.

Concerns mean they would like to do it, but they need your help clearing up some issues.

Objections are telling you there is a negative issue.

If you ignore their objections, or don't actively seek out objections (*what are you thinking right now?*), you run the risk of the customer shutting you off. They may no longer be listening to you.

Objections are not a problem, they are a part of human behavior. Objections are a normal step in the psychological process. As people (and our prospects are people) transition from meeting a complete stranger to making an important purchase, they have to go through various psychological steps, and if they have any doubt – then objections are part of that process.

In fact, in most sales scenarios the customer is going to have to explain and justify this purchase recommendation or decision to another person or group of people. Many times they are repeating the objections of others, or anticipating the objections that others might have.

Here's a very interesting point about human psychology. Many times a person is IMAGINING that other people are watching. He imagines what his boss will say. He imagines what his neighbors/church members/co-workers will say. He imagines what his wife will say. He imagines what his kids will say.

He is actually expressing a concern or an objection based on how he thinks this imaginary audience will judge his decision. So psychologically, he has to express these concerns. These concerns have to be addressed as part of the decision process.

This is perfectly normal.

Here's a true story. My 22 year old daughter came home for a weekend and we were talking. She mentioned that she had an opportunity to take a part time job. I asked her why she didn't take the job, it sounded interesting. She told me that she decided not to take the job because she thought I would have preferred her to focus on her classes during her last semester, rather than spend time on this job.

She was imagining what I was going to think. She made a decision based on her imagination of me looking over her shoulder.

We all have this imaginary audience and we unconsciously measure our actions and decisions against what we think would meet their approval. If a customer actually tells you they are worried about what their husband/wife/children/neighbors/co-workers, etc. might say – handle it like this:

> *"What will you say to your (husband/wife/children/neighbors/co-workers, etc.) when they tell you they don't like this decision?"*

> *"I'll tell them it's my decision, not theirs."*

Imaginary audience objection handled.

IF YOU CAN COUNT TO THREE – YOU CAN HANDLE OBJECTIONS

As a professional, you understand that there will be objections. This is normal human behavior. You are not surprised or upset by the objection, but rather completely prepared and ready to work with the customer through the objection and turn it around to your advantage.

When you hear an objection, the very next thing you say is critical. **Remember 1, 2, 3**.

1. **Agree**
2. **Paraphrase**
3. **Ask Questions to Uncover More Information**

Agree and Paraphrase

"OK. I understand. You think (then reflect or paraphrase the objection) (the price is too high) (your boss will never go for this) (this doesn't have enough memory capacity for your application) (this is way out of your budget) (you're not allowed to buy anything from a new vendor) (you don't trust our company because we haven't been in business long enough) (this is not something that you would use) (etc.). I certainly understand. You need to be 100% comfortable with this decision. I certainly understand."

Now get more detail behind the objection by asking.

> *You say the price is too high. What do you mean by that?*
> *What makes you say...?*
> *Can you explain that in a little more detail?*
> *What else are you concerned about?*
> *I'm getting the sense that there are several things bothering you. What is the real issue that is concerning you? What else? What else?*

These questions will lead you to the real reasons for their discomfort – and usually it boils down to only one major concern. Even when there are multiple concerns, when you knock down their biggest concern they tend to be much more receptive. The chemistry is changed from that point forward.

They may not be able to buy this, or it may not be a good fit. These questions will help you see the whole story – from the customer's perspective – and lead you to the best path to either resolve their concerns or move on.

If handled well, objections disarm the emotion, make the customer feel more comfortable, and will lead to questions.

Here's a true personal story. I was at a trade show and walked up to a booth and thought these guys would be a good potential customer. I started chatting with the salesperson and when I told him the product / service I offered he pointed to a man who was sitting three feet away typing into his laptop. He had heard everything I had said. The salesperson pointed and said, *"this is our CEO. He's the guy you would need to talk to."*

Without looking up from his laptop he said, *"I'm not interested. We already get everything from ABC company and they do a great job for us."*

Remember 1, 2, 3:

"I completely understand. You have a great relationship with ABC and you're getting everything you need from them. Let me ask you this, what would it take to give some of your business to me?"

"What company are you with again?"

And that's all I needed!

This technique truly works!

Avoid the Urge to Prove Your Point

When they state an objection they are now psychologically leaning away from you. You can only pull them back towards you by agreeing and asking questions – giving them the opportunity to express all their concerns. When they feel listened to, they will psychologically lean back towards you and be able to listen to you.

But if you come straight out and disagree with them and throw your list of facts and bullet points at them to prove your point they will psychologically pull further back from you.

The harder you try to convince me that you're right, the more I think you're wrong.

Be 100% Prepared for Objections

The truth is that most salespeople hear about five or six of the same objections over and over. You know what they are going to be. A professional salesperson simply prepares for these objections. He knows what the objections will be, and he knows his responses – by heart.

I encourage you to create index cards for every objection. On one side of the card write down the objection, and on the other side write down all the bullet points you can cover to turn that objection around. In addition to objections you can also make a card for each of your competitors, so when they mention a competitor you have point by point information at your fingertips.

Also, keep a daily log of all the objections you hear, or write them on your whiteboard or pin them on the wall. There are a hundred different ways that a customer says the price is too high, or they are concerned about the warranty, or whatever the objection. Each time you hear an objection keep it in your notebook or on your whiteboard. This will help you become comfortable with objections, be able to quickly classify them into specific categories, and will help you realize that objections are perfectly normal and are part of the sales process.

After You Have Uncovered All Their Concerns

After you have allowed them to speak about their concerns, and you have asked even more questions, now is when you want to have your index cards ready.

So your main concern is the longevity of our company, is that right?

So your main concern is that this is simply beyond your budget, is that right?

So your main concern is that you had a bad experience with us in the past, is that right?

Well let me address that...

Now is the time to use the Feel/Felt/Found formula for handling objections.

I understand exactly how you <u>feel</u>, a lot of our customers were concerned about our company's longevity and our ability to stand behind the warranty. They <u>felt</u> this was so important that it was the key criteria in their buying decision. We had the best product and the best value, but without the company around in five years, the warranty would be useless. What they <u>found</u> was that...

Anticipating Objections Early in the Process

The more you understand, classify and dissect objections, the more you can anticipate objections and address them earlier in the process. There should be no real surprises, you should already know what the most common objections are, and incorporate these types of statements into your early conversation.

For example, if you're selling appliances – you already know that people are trying to find the lowest price, so they will get a price from you then go to the other appliance stores in the area and shop for the lowest price. Or you may hear them state it bluntly: "I can get a lower price from ABC Appliances across the street."

You know it's coming, so early in your conversation you completely disarm the objection:

"While we're looking at these different models, I want to make sure you know about our Low Price Guarantee. We actually will go on the internet with you and look for a lower price from any of our local competitors. Whatever their price is, we will match it. Does that sound fair?"

If you're a home remodeler, you already know that people will want to talk to references and see samples of your work. Simply bring your photo book with work samples and references. By making it a part of your presentation you are eliminating the objection later on.

Everyone gets the price objection, so simply say something that sets them up to be pleasantly surprised when you tell them the price.

"Some people get sticker shock when they see our price, and then other people are skeptical that we don't charge enough. Either way, they have found that considering everything we include, it's really a very fair – even a great price. Let me tell you what's included."

Typically you will have five or six common objections which come up all the time. Many of these can be handled up front. The others you should have a memorized list of things to say every time this comes up – of course, after you have agreed, paraphrased, listened and asked questions to get more information.

Other Methods for Handling Objections

I personally believe that my three-step method for handling objections is the best I've found. I have done a lot of research on various methods for handling objections, and I still believe this method works best.

1. **Agree**
2. **Paraphrase**
3. **Uncover more information**

This is the method I use and it works for me.

"We already have a vendor who handles those products for us."

"I certainly understand. You have a good relationship with another vendor. I appreciate that. Let me ask you a question, what would have to exist for you to give us some of your business?"

Sometimes they will say *"No way."* I thank them for their time and move on. Other times they will say, *"Well, if your price was better that would be a consideration."* That's my opportunity!

While my 1, 2, 3 method works for me all the time, I did want to share other ideas about objection handling, because there are different types of sales personalities, different types of products, and different types of sales scenarios, and some of these other ideas may be helpful in your situation.

Defer the Objection

The first and the simplest suggestion is to defer the objection.

"That's a great question, and if it's ok I will address that later."

Of course, later the chemistry of the meeting is different and that objection may no longer be an issue. Many objections may be completely eliminated if you simply defer them to later.

Isolate the Objection

"OK. I understand. You think the price is too high. Price aside, is that the only concern you have or are there other concerns?"

This is actually a pre-closing technique because after you have addressed this objection you are now going to use the customer's own words against him, and not allow him to bring up other objections.

Some people believe that by asking the customer for his list of concerns you are giving up control of the conversation and allowing the customer to take control, and you are getting further and further away from a close. I have a different opinion. I want to have a relationship with the customer, and a relationship implies that I value their thoughts and opinions and I genuinely want to make this work for them.

I think hard sell techniques (coming up next) are not in line with understanding and working with customer behavior. I want to allow the customer to resolve all his concerns. I don't need to trick him into limiting his concerns to only one.

Ask questions like:

"It seems like you have several concerns. What's really on your mind?"

"You seem troubled. What is your main concern?"

Power Through the Objection Directly to a Close

This one really goes against my personal selling philosophy, but I present it here because it certainly seems to work for some salespeople.

The thought is that if you very strongly believe in your product, and you know the customer will benefit, you are not going to allow him to say "no". With this philosophy, you treat objections as closing opportunities. You're not gathering more information about the customer's objection, you're "powering through the objection," and closing the deal right then.

"I want to think about it." (an objection we will cover in a separate chapter)

The "Power Through the Objection" philosophy would have you say something like this:

"I understand Mr. Customer – you need to think about it. Suppose you think about this for three hours, or three days, or three weeks, or three months. No matter how long you think about it you're still going to come down to this fundamental decision point, aren't you? Let's go ahead and do this."

"This is really more than I can afford at the present moment."

Powering through the objection would go something like this:

"I understand Mr. Customer - $99/month is a lot of money. But aren't you worth it? Isn't your (safety/wife/sense of luxury, etc.) worth a mere $3/day? Let's go ahead and do this – you won't regret it."

As you can see, this is a very different approach from agreeing and asking questions to uncover more detail. This is literally – powering through the objection to a close.

This is not my philosophy, but I present it to you because it does suit some salespeople.

Flipping the BUT

Help Them Resolve Their Concerns

Here's the Definition of a Concern:

When a customer wants to buy your product or service, but something, or some factor, or some circumstance, or some lack of knowledge, or some person is holding them back.

By using <u>Trial Close</u> questions, you will discover their concerns and hesitations.

Sometimes they will come right out and tell you:

"I really like your product, in fact I think it's better than what we're using now, BUT it's more expensive than our current solution and there's no way we can add to the budget."

"I wish I could move forward, BUT the timing is off."

"I like this service, I see the benefits, BUT my boss would never go for it."

"I can see how this would work, BUT we don't want to be the guinea pig. Go get some other people to try it first."

"I like it, BUT I'm afraid what my (neighbors, spouse, church members) would think."

BUT, BUT, BUT.

Everyone I know has a big BUT. And it's always a negative BUT.

<u>Trial Close</u> questions help us uncover everyone's big BUT.

BUT is a very powerful word, BUT unfortunately it's a very negative word. We use it all the time to stop people, or ourselves, from moving forward.

When you analyze these BUT statements, you'll see the first part of the sentence gets overwhelmed by the second part. All we hear is the second part – after the BUT.

"I wish I could stay late and help you with this report, BUT I have other commitments tonight."

The wish is that I could stay and help, the reality is that I'm leaving early, and you're on your own.

The wish is that I could buy your product or service, the reality is that I can't.

The wish is that I could afford your product or service, the reality is that I can't.

"This is really good report card, BUT I'm concerned about this C in math."

"You're a great employee, BUT we are concerned about your recent sick days."

The first part of the sentence – before the BUT - is overwhelmed by the second part of the sentence.

Sometimes your customers will clearly articulate their concerns in this way. *"I want to do it, BUT for reasons A, B and C, I can't."* Other times your customer does not say it this clearly. They may not tell you how much they like it, but instead they list all the negatives.

"My boss will never go for this."
"This isn't in the budget."
"My husband would never approve."
"We don't buy from unapproved vendors."
"We've already made a decision."

The hidden fact is that they would really like to do it. So you ask this question:

> "Forgetting external factors for a minute, do you think it will be beneficial?"
> "If it were in the budget, would you recommend it?"
> "If we were an approved vendor, would this solution solve your problem?" "Well yes it would, BUT I can't even consider it because you are not an approved vendor."

Other times your customer will repeat the positive and misleads you into thinking that everything is going great... This is great. This is fantastic. This is perfect. This is amazing. BUT they don't move forward. When they are really positive, BUT they can't move forward – it is almost always because they are imagining what other people will say. They have a series of imaginary people watching them and they don't want to make a decision that these people (boss, husband, wife, neighbor, co-worker, church member) will not approve. So your job is to uncover those concerns.

Again, it is up to you to uncover those concerns with great Trial Close questions, follow-up questions, and listening.

When you hear a CONCERN - boil it down to the **BUT formula.**

"We would like to do this, BUT we can't because of A, B and C."

Whether explicitly or implicitly – they are telling you they want to do this, BUT they have concerns which are preventing them from doing this.

Now here's the **FLIP THE BUT** technique. Flip the second part of the sentence before the BUT, and put the first part of the sentence last.

> "So you're concerned about A, B and C, BUT you would really like to move forward, right?" "Yes."

"So you don't think your boss will approve it, BUT you think this is the right thing to do, right?" "Yes."
"So you don't have the budget for this, BUT you believe this is better than your current solution, right?"
"So you're concerned about what other people might think, BUT as far as you're concerned you believe this product or service is the right thing to do, right?"

By flipping the BUT, the second part of the statement now has priority over the first part. Flipping the BUT has the effect of diminishing their concerns, and emphasizing their desire to move forward.

Now you engage in problem solving.

"OK, so let's look at some ways we can address A, B and C."
"OK, so let's talk a little bit about how to present this to your boss. What's most important to her?"
"OK, so let's see if there is a way to get this into your budget, or to defer the payment into next month's budget."
"OK, so what will you say to your (husband/wife, neighbors, co-workers, church members) when they tell you they don't approve of you buying this?"

The key to this technique is to become an expert at the Trial Close. You need to be skilled at drawing out a customer's state of mind – either interest, concern, or objection.

If they are interested – that's easy – you move the process along to an eventual, or a quick close.

If they want to move forward but have concerns, you need to ask more questions, and draw out more details – let them tell you their concerns. Sometimes their concerns are easily addressed by returning to your presentation – *"That's a great point – I was going to cover that."* Other times you can address their concerns with the Flip the BUT technique.

The Flip the BUT Technique allows you to turn their concerns into problem solving dialog.

You can always use the 1, 2, 3 formula for handling objections, BUT the Flip the BUT Technique can be used when the customer says they are actually interested, BUT...

Practice this a few times (flip a few BUTs), and it becomes another arrow in your communications / influence quiver.

Loss Statements Can Save a Sale

My entire philosophy of selling is to help lead the customer to the very best solution for them – even if I make less money. Obviously, if I treat people right, and keep their interests ahead of my own, they will come back to me over and over again, recommend me and open up new opportunities. Always do what's best for the customer – it pays off.

But there are situations where you will need to guide a customer to your recommendation. The most important examples are "all or nothing" situations where you are about to lose the sale. For example, when the customer tells you they are going to go with your competitor, or they simply are not going to move forward with you.

Loss Statements can help you SAVE THE SALE. They are also a way to guide a customer to one decision or another, or to get over the hump and make a decision to move forward.

Psychologically, people react more strongly to a fear of losing rather than a promise of saving.

For example, if I tell you that I can save you $10/month – you have a mildly positive reaction – "that's nice." But if I flip it and tell you that if you don't work with me you will lose $10 every month, there is a psychological pull because you don't want to lose something.

It sounds silly when it's explained here, but try it on the phone or when you are in person with a client.

Here's an example: Your customer is leaning toward your competitor. The competitor has a good solution, but let's say in this case your advantage is your warranty and superior level of service.

Savings Statement

> *"Remember, we offer a stronger warranty and we have the highest level of service in the industry."*

Loss Statement

> *"Those guys offer a good product for sure, but keep in mind that you will be losing access to our service after the sale and our stronger warranty. You don't want to lose that, you know?"*

Here is some generic wording of a Loss Statement:
> *"There are definitely other companies that can offer this same service and maybe even at a lower price, but keep in mind that you would be losing...."*

The loss statement has the psychological effect of pulling the customer back and keeping the conversation alive. This is not to say that every customer will stay with you every time, but the fact that most people react to a loss statement will allow you to at least keep the conversation going which, of course, allows you to revisit their concerns and their needs and take another shot at it.

Once you keep the customer conversation going, move to your objection handling technique – ask a question. *"Obviously you're still not completely comfortable. What are you main concerns?"*

Try this on a customer who is definitely not going to use your product/service. *"I understand you're not going to be moving ahead with us. I just hate to see you losing..."* From a psychological perspective, **it is very difficult for someone to hang up the phone on a loss statement**. See how it works – you have nothing to lose, and more importantly, you can save the sale!

Using a Loss Statement to Help a Customer Make a Decision

It's decision time. Your customer has heard the pitch but they are still on the fence.

Let's say in this example you're selling an Energy Audit for $750.

> *"I understand your hesitation. It's a lot of money, and you want to make sure you're making the right decision. I understand."* (Perfect Objection Handling- Agree and Paraphrase)

> Notice the difference in the next two statements – a Savings/Benefits Statement vs. a Loss Statement.

Savings Statement

> *"As we discussed, the savings we identify in this Energy Audit are going to save you $70 to $80/month on your electric bill."*

No. That's ok. I'm fine.

Loss Statement

> *"As we discussed, if you don't go ahead with this Energy Audit, you will be losing $70 to $80 every single month on your electric bill."*

Many times you will get a yes right on the spot, but at the very least the loss statement will keep the conversation going which will give you more opportunity to identify concerns, and build enough value in the customer's mind.

> *"Are you ready to move forward?"*
>
> If no...
>
> *"OK, I understand. Tell me what you're concerned about."*

Using Loss Statements in Consultative Mode to Encourage a Choice

If you're in consultative mode and you are working through two different options, you can normally guide them to your preferred option if you word the alternatives with "loss" in mind.

> "I think we have pretty much narrowed it down to these two choices..."

A real estate agent presenting two houses:

> "House A will definitely save you money, but you will be losing the extra closet space and the larger kitchen and family room that you get in House B."

Human nature pulls the clients back to House B because they don't want to lose anything.

> "The Silver plan is great. It gets you A, B, C and D – just keep in mind you're losing two very important features E and F that you get on the Gold Plan."

> "The X1000 will definitely be the least expensive option, but just keep in mind that you're losing the extra capacity of the X3000, future upgradability, and the ability to log in remotely."

The Price Objection

It's Really a Buying Signal

The price objection is not really an objection – it is a BUYING SIGNAL. He's going to buy it – he's just making it very clear that he may or may not buy it from you. He's negotiating for him to keep more of his money, and for you to keep less of yours.

This is the most common objection you will hear. As a professional you need to be completely prepared for this – in fact, look forward to the objection as a chance to turn the conversation toward a close, and hit it out of the park. Your friends and co-workers will be amazed, but all you did was prepare.

There is a school of thought – quite correct as far as it goes – that you should never get a price objection. The thinking is that if you have asked enough questions and thoroughly understood their needs, and you have worked with them through the process of selecting the right product(s) to fit their needs, and showed the value of your solution as it addresses their exact needs, and verified with them every step of the way – that the sale just naturally progresses to the close. Like I said, that's great as far as it goes. But even the best salesman will get compared to his competition from time to time, and will be told that his price is too high.

There's another school of thought that you should not bother with customers who price you against your competition. If they don't recognize your superior quality, or see the additional value in your level of service then you don't want them as customers. Let them go buy at a lower price from a less reputable company, and they will come back hat in hand. I totally disagree. You want these customers, and you want to be able to get them even though you may be a little higher than the competition. You want them to understand your value.

Example: Here's the price objection. You will hear this all the time.

"Your price is too high. I can get this somewhere else for less."

Here are some prepared responses. Of course, you need to create your own responses which are appropriate for your situation.

So you're saying you can buy this somewhere else for less. I completely understand.

- Tell me a little bit more about what you mean when you say our price is too high.
- Tell me a little more about the prices you're finding out there.
- Let me find out if I have any room on the price here. If I can do something with the price, do we have a deal?
- I know exactly how you feel. I'm a price shopper myself. If I can find something cheaper I usually go for that option myself. What are you seeing on the market? Show me the details or send me a link to my competitor's web page so I can make sure it's apples to apples. If we can match a competitor's price, can we move forward?
- I understand that our price may not be the lowest. Our customers appreciate our level of service and how we stand behind our products. It may not be the first time or the second time, but after you order from us a few times you will come to understand why it may be worth a few extra dollars to order from us instead of some

anonymous company on eBay. That makes sense, don't you think?

- We are definitely not a bargain basement company. I'm sure the company you are pricing us against is reputable, but with eBay and Google and Amazon, these days anybody out there can put one of these for sale. Our advantage is our service, and that's why we may end up being a few dollars more. You might be able to get it cheaper somewhere, but you won't find a company who stands behind the product after the sale to the level that we do, you know?

- Wow! Normally we are competitive, most of the time our prices are aggressive. Are we comparing apples to apples? We take our pricing very seriously, and while we offer better warranty and service after the sale, we still take pride on being competitively priced. Can I see their quote, or can you link me to a website showing that price? (then he shows you the website). OK if it's apples to apples and I can match that price do we have a deal?

- Wow! Is their warranty the same? When are they saying they can deliver – we can deliver this tomorrow. Do they have strong tech support after the sale? Our tech support team is world class, and that's what's really important, isn't it?

- If the price is too high, maybe we can look at another model which might be more in line with your budget.

Let Me Think it Over

This is the death phrase for many salespeople. They know once the customer leaves or hangs up the phone – they will never hear from them again. The customer has listened, asked questions, understood – and now is making a reasonable request to think it over for a few days.

By understanding human nature you recognize this objection as a BUYING SIGNAL. If handled correctly, this statement will lead to the sale far more often than not.

Here's why this is a positive signal. Because **in the language of human nature "Let me think this over" really means "I can definitely see myself doing this**, but I'm just not sure."

They can see themselves doing this, but they have some doubts about something.

You treat this just like any other objection.

1. Agree
2. Paraphrase
3. Ask Questions to Uncover Their Concerns

Let me think about this for a few days.

> Sure. I understand. I want you to be 100% confident with this decision. What are going to be the most important issues that you will be thinking about, and where do we stand on those right now? If I can ask, what are you unsure of?

Let me think about this for a few days.

Sure I understand. You're not sure one way or the other. If you did this, what would be your main concern?

Let me think about this for a few days.

Sure I understand. This is a very important decision and you're not sure one way or the other. What are your main concerns right now?

Let me think about this and we'll get back to you.

Sure I understand. Let me ask. What's making you uncomfortable right now?

Don't convince him that he needs to make a decision now or use some gimmick statement or close.

DO NOT schedule a follow-up appointment in a week. Use the 1, 2, 3 formula for Objection Handling to keep the conversation going and moving toward a close.

Agree, paraphrase, and ask questions to uncover their discomfort(s), and move toward the tie-down.

Practice Makes Perfect

Handling Objections Like a Pro

I was watching a documentary one Saturday afternoon. They were interviewing pilots who had landed their plane under extreme circumstances. You remember "Sully" the pilot who landed his plane in the Hudson River off New York City, and stayed on the plane until over 200 passengers were evacuated safely.

One of the pilots had a large hole in the fuselage at 30,000 feet. One of the pilots couldn't get his landing gear to open, etc.

It was all very interesting.

They asked one of the pilots:

"What were you thinking at that moment?"

And the pilot immediately responded:

"I had gone through that exact situation a hundred times in a flight simulator. **At that moment I'm not paid to think, I'm paid to react."**

Wow! He had practiced and practiced and practiced emergency situations hundreds of times. When the emergency came, he simply reverted to his training, he reacted instantly and saved the lives of hundreds of people.

You can do the same thing with Objections. Don't be surprised, or hurt, or disappointed by an objection – be 100% prepared. Don't think about your response, simply react with the best response.

You're price is too high. I can get it cheaper from several of your competitors.

I'll have to run this by my boss to get his approval.

Let me think about it.

There's no way we could afford this type of expense right now.

Etc.

When you're brushing your teeth in the morning, driving in your car to work, eating lunch – repeat a hundred times every day!

You're price is too high.

Prepare your response using the 1, 2, 3 formula for Handling Objections, then repeat your answer a hundred times a day.

Like the pilot who practices emergency situations a hundred times on a flight simulator – practice each objection a hundred times a day.

Then, like they do every time, your customer is going to say, *"You know I can get this cheaper from one of your competitors."* BOOM you have your response completely prepared.

Prepare yourself to the point where you can just react. This is a softball – I was 100% ready for this one, and now I'm going to hit it out of the park.

Objections

Common Questions

Cold Call opening statements

Features and Benefits

Differences from your competition

Come up with the best information, then practice, practice, practice, drill, drill drill.

As a professional, take the time to prepare yourself. Then when the situations come up you are 100% ready.

Practice really does make perfect!

I Need to Talk About This With My Partner

Oops. You made a very common mistake. It happens to every salesperson, so don't fear. But this is a situation you need to learn to avoid.

You have given your presentation, they loved it.

"This sounds great, but I'll need to run this by my partner (wife/husband/boss/manager/CEO)."

You have given your presentation without the decision maker present. Even worse, you've given your presentation without understanding their decision process.

As you become more experienced in sales, you must learn to ask this question up front.

Here is the question that most people are taught to ask: "Who is the decision maker?"

While it's better than not asking, it's not a great question. This can only be answered with a single name, so many people will simply identify themselves as the decision maker, when in fact they are not. Or they may identify one person, who in fact is also not the decision maker.

A Better Question:

**"Can you walk me through your decision process?"
"How do you (or How does your company) normally make a decision like this?"**

This begins a conversation which allows you to ask more questions about how the decisions are made, what level has budget authority, whose budget is this coming from, the timing, the criteria being considered for this decision, other alternatives they are considering, what competitors have been invited to present a proposal, etc.

In order of preference – from strongest position to weakest position:

1. Only present when all the stakeholders, all the decision makers, are in the room.
2. If necessary, present to the gatekeeper, then do the next presentation to the decision makers.
3. Present to the gatekeeper, then they take the information back to the decision maker.
4. You forgot to ask about the decision process, and you have already presented – then you find out that the person you presented to was not the decision maker. (You can still recover from this, but it is something you should work to make sure doesn't happen frequently.)

If you get the inside scoop on the decision process and all the people who need to be involved, you can work to get everyone invited to your presentation.

> *"OK. What's the best way to get everyone together to hear about this solution?"*

You might get pushback – *"You need to present this to me, then I will present it to our CEO."*

If you get this pushback, you need to be assertive:

> *"I'm sure you understand our process. From a cost point of view, and to save time, our process works best when we present this to all the stakeholders. How can we make that happen?"*

> *"It will be much more efficient and effective if we could have everyone in the room for the presentation. How can we make that happen?"*

You have been assertive and tried to defend your right to present only to the decision maker.

You may still get pushback.

> *"Here is how our process works. You present your product/service to me, then I bring it back to the team for consideration."*

> *"OK well let me ask you if I will get the opportunity, after presenting this to you, to present again to the team – because that would be the most effective way to make sure they get all their questions and concerns answered."*

Since you can't present to all the decision makers up front, you try to at least get to give the next presentation – rather than rely on this person to present it for you.

Other times you arrive for your appointment, and the decision maker turns out to be out that day.

Now you are in position 2 or 3. You are giving your presentation to a person who is not the final decision maker. What's the best way to proceed?

Now is where we do our best Needs Development work.

> *"Since your (partner/boss/CEO/husband/wife) is not here, what are the things that are most important to them? What are their decision criteria? What are their main concerns? What other solutions do they like, or don't like?"*

Try to learn as much as possible about the decision makers needs, concerns, preferences, past experiences – so that you can tailor your presentation to not only the person in the room with you, but the other stakeholders and the decision maker who are not there with you.

Now the 4th situation is the weakest situation. While it does happen to all of us from time to time, we all need to get stronger in asking about the decision process up-front. Not waiting until after we have already given our presentation.

But, like I said, it happens to all of us from time to time, so what's the best way to get yourself out of this weak position?

> *"Wow. This is a great solution, but I'm going to need to talk to my partner (husband/wife/boss/CEO, etc.) and get their input."*

This is the textbook example of [Handling an Objection with the 1, 2, 3 formula](#).

> *"Sure. I understand. You need to talk to your partner before moving ahead. This is a very important decision, and you want to make sure you are both on the same page. I understand."*

You can also use a ["Flip the But"](#) technique.

> *"OK I understand. You need to talk to your partner, but if it were up to you – you would move ahead, right?"*

Now do Needs Development.

> *So tell me a little bit about your partner, what is going to be most important to him/her?*
>
> *How do they make a decision like this?*
>
> *Based on what you heard just now, what would be their reaction?*
>
> *What would they be concerned about?*
>
> *How do you resolve a decision when you disagree?*
>
> *Etc.*
>
> *When can <u>the three of us</u> meet to go through this presentation again?*

It happens to all of us from time to time. It's not a good situation to be in.

But remember to work hard during the up-front process to learn about their decision process, present to all the decision makers, and when that's not possible, to explore the needs of the decision maker and all the stakeholders so you can address those issues during your presentation.

Questions and Tie-Downs

Questions Are a Sign of Interest

Questions are buying signals. Questions are different than objections. Questions are an expression of interest, they want more information, they are psychologically leaning forward. I love questions – that means I'm going to make a sale today. Objections mean I've got more work to do. Objections are a sign of hesitation and concern, psychologically leaning backward. There may not be a good fit here – I need to explore the reason behind the objection.

Questions are buying signals. If I wasn't interested, I would be telling you I wasn't interested. I would not be asking you for more information.

What about your warranty?

Does this come in a larger size?

What if I don't like it after I buy it?

What is your return policy?

How many of these have you installed?

Who else is doing this?

Where is your manufacturing facility?

How long have you guys been in business?

Can I combine this with the other item and get a discount?

Do you have any references I can contact?

Are you guys able to drop ship to a different location?

How does lowering the quantity affect the price?

Try this from now on – every time you hear a question.

Questions are a signal that you can try to close the sale. Obviously, some sales situations are longer and you don't move to a close right away – but questions ARE a sign of interest and represent an opportunity to move closer.

Rather than simply answering the question, give an answer AND ALSO use a tie-down question or statement.

Can you come down on the price?
Standard Answer: Let me check.
Answer Plus Tie-Down: Let me check. If I can do something with the price are we good to go?

What about your warranty?
Standard Answer: Ok let me bring out the warranty.
Answer Plus Tie-Down: Let me go get you a copy of our warranty. Do you want the 3-year or the 5-year warranty? If the warranty checks out are we good to go?

Here's another great answer to this question:

Tell me about your warranty?
Standard Answer: We have a great warranty. It covers A, B and C.
Answer Plus Tie-Down: That is a great question because we're going to be doing a lot of business together in the future – so it's very important that you fully understand…

Can I return this if I don't like it?
Standard Answer: Absolutely.
Answer Plus Tie-Down: Absolutely. Are we delivering this to your home, or are you going to drive around back and put in your car right now?

Does this come in a larger size?
Standard Answer: Absolutely.

Answer Plus Tie-Down: Let me check my inventory. If we have the larger one in stock, when do you need it delivered?

Can I combine this with the other item and get a discount?
Standard Answer: Yes we can do that.

Answer Plus Tie-Down: If I can create a package deal, will that do it for you?

Do you have any references I can call?
Standard Answer: Absolutely. I will email you a list of references – you'll have it when you get back to your office.

Answer Plus Tie-Down: Absolutely. Assuming the references check out, are we ready to move forward?

"We're Not Buying Today"

How to Handle This Situation

How do you deal with the customer who tells you right in the beginning of the meeting that they are not making a decision today? They are not buying today. They are just gathering information. They are just shopping.

From the customer's point of view – they have made a decision. Their decision is that they are not going to make a decision today. They have decided not to commit.

If you have been in sales for more than a week, you have heard this. It is very common in all types of sales.

As we discuss this challenging situation, it brings us to understand an important point about customer psychology, and it also leads us to advanced closing techniques.

It's easy enough to prepare a response to the "we're just shopping" scenario.

"No problem. That will allow us to get a broad overview of our solution and get all your questions answered. Is that what you were expecting from this meeting?"

Or

"I understand. Most people who come here are just interested in seeing what we have to offer and gathering information. That's fine. I can show you around and maybe point out a few things that are on sale or that might be a good fit for you. Is that what you had in mind for today?"

Or

"I understand. Today will be just for learning and gathering information. That actually takes the pressure off because we can focus on giving you the big picture and getting all your questions answered. Is that what you had in mind for today?"

This completely disarms the customer and allows you to easily move into building rapport and Needs Development questions.

"Before we jump in, let me ask you a few questions..."

So far, pretty easy.

As the process continues, you help the customer discover that your product / solution is a perfect fit.

It's all going well. They love it. They want it. They see the value of it. They ask great questions. Buying signals are flying left and right.

Let's pause here and review several different strategies that a salesperson can use at this point.

Weak Salesperson

OK Great. You really like this solution. So, what's the next step?

What did he do wrong? A weak salesperson is excited that the customer loves the product/solution. He thinks he's got them. But he makes the huge mistake of putting the control back into the customer's hands by asking them to identify the next step.

The customer will almost always say the same thing:

Yeah, this is really great.

Can I have your card?

Can we get a brochure?

We'll call you when we're ready. Do you get paid on commission? Don't worry. We will definitely be buying this from you.

Sometimes a weak salesperson gets lucky and the customer will close themselves, but 90% of the time the customer will delay their decision to a later date.

Average Salesperson

The average salesperson at this point will try to close.

"OK Great. You really like this product/solution. Let me go ahead and get the paperwork started."

Not bad, but the customer will still respond that they are only shopping (or not making a decision) today and they'll ask for a brochure and a business card.

"We'll call you back when we're ready."

Or…

"We were pretty clear. We're not going to do anything today. We're just gathering information right now."

You've built great rapport with the customer, you've done a great job at Needs Development, and you did a great job presenting your product/solution and got them sold.

But they leave, and you are not getting a real shot at closing the deal.

I call this the "Pity Goodbye Wave" or the "Pity Goodbye Handshake" as you say:

"Goodbye. It was really nice meeting you. I'll send you a follow up email then we'll be in touch in a few months."

Their earlier decision to *"not make a decision today"* is stronger than your ability to close them on making a decision today.

You've heard the saying, *"someone is always getting sold."* Either you're selling them on closing, or they're selling you on not buying today.

Unfortunately in this scenario everyone loses. Obviously you and your company lose because you didn't make the sale, but also the customer has lost. They are leaving without a product/service they love.

The Impossible Sale

You quickly realize that this is an impossible sale!

They tell you up front that they are not going to buy today, and it's very easy for them to follow through on that decision – and walk away.

The only way to solve this problem is to understand Customer Psychology.

Here's how the psychology works.

At the very beginning of the sales call, the customer has already made a decision. *"I'm not buying (or making a decision) today."*

I recognize this psychological state in my own behavior. When I am walking in a mall with my wife and a salesman comes out of a kiosk and asks *"Have you seen the Gizmo 5000?"* or *"Would you like a free vacation?"* or anything they say – I immediately say to myself *"I'm not buying this in a million years."* It is an instantaneous resistive instinct. We don't want to be sold.

I don't give them eye contact, I don't smile. But then my wife moves over and starts talking to the salesman. I know she can hear me loud and clear through mental telepathy *"Honey, we're not buying this. Let's move on."* She glances over and she can see my body language and a scowl on my face and she knows exactly what I'm thinking.

No matter what you're selling, this is a decision that many of your customers have made even before the conversation starts. This resistive mindset - *"I'm not buying today"* - is ingrained in their mind. They are willing to listen to your message, but they are going to resist any movement toward a sale.

This psychology is very important to understand, because think about what we're asking our customers to do.

> We're asking them to throw away the instinctive decision they have already made, completely reverse themselves and make a new, opposite decision to move forward. We're asking them to make a commitment on the fly, with no planning or preparation.

We have to build a bridge for them to cross from "no" to "yes".

This is actually a very common sales scenario. Financial Planners send out post cards inviting people to a free dinner at a local restaurant. Time Share resorts offer a free bottle of wine if you sit through their presentation. Anyone who is offering anything for "free" is capturing your attention, knowing that you start out with the mindset that you are not buying.

It's fairly easy to get people receptive to listening to your message, to accepting the information you have to share – but they will naturally be resistant to your effort to get them to move forward. So while it seems like you're making progress, you have great rapport, they love you and your product/service – when push comes to shove – they're sticking with their instinct. *"I'm not buying (or making a decision) today."*

Now that we understand the psychology, how do we overcome it to a successful close?

There are a few strategies you can employ in the beginning of the sales process.

Strategy: Cancel or disarm this objection IN THE BEGINNING of the sales call.

"I know you already have another solution..."

"I know you're just looking today..."

"I know this was the last thing on your mind when you woke up today..."

Etc.

Here's how it might sound.

"I know you weren't planning on making a decision today, so I really appreciate you taking the time to see what we have to offer. Thank you for keeping an open mind."

"I hear you loud and clear. You're just gathering information today. No problem."

So in the customer's mind: *"Finally, a salesperson who understands that I'm just shopping."*

Strategy: Tell them that a lot of people have trouble making a commitment, even after they have found the right solution. Do this as you begin your needs development questions.

Here's how it might sound. *"Help me understand what you're looking for. I want to understand this from your perspective, through your eyes. Everybody has a different set of needs and priorities, and some people have difficulty making a commitment even after they have found the perfect solution. So where are you in the process? What research have you done so far?"*

The 180° Close or The Impossible Close or The Big Boy Close

Here's the close. It's a step by step process to get the customer to go from *"not today"* to *"tell me more."*

You've done all your steps. You've asked great questions, you've built a trust relationship, you've presented your product/service by showing how it meets their needs, wants and goals, and you've explained the unique advantages of your product/service and your company.

They understand it. They like it. They recognize the value. They even want it.

But they are not closed. They still want to walk away.

I call it The 180° Close because you are going to flip them 180° from their original decision not to buy today.

I call it The Impossible Close because you are going to get them to completely reverse their decision to resist the sale.

I call it The Big Boy Close because this is where the Big Boy Salespeople separate themselves from everyone else.

At this point always take the following two steps:

1. **Summarize and Confirm** that you have met their needs and buying criteria by repeating back to them what they told you was important

   "You said your solution needed to have A, B, C. Check, check, check. So this product/service meets all those criteria, right?"

2. **Ask for the Sale** – very straightforward: *"I'd like to go ahead and get this written up (or get started, or get this rolling). Does that sound like a plan?"*

   Or Alternative Choice:

   "I'd like to get the paperwork started so you can get the benefit right away. Would you like it delivered on Thursday or Friday?"

When you ask for the sale:

- Some will move forward.
- Most will say no for fear of making a decision or a commitment.

"We're not ready to make a decision right now."

"We were pretty clear. We're not making a decision today."

"We're not going to make a decision until June of next year."

"We need to do more research."

"We're going to stay with what we have right now."

"We're still in the process of looking at all our options. We'll let you know if we're interested."

The vast majority of salespeople simply say: *"Ok. When would be the best time to get back to you?"*

But the Big Boys – the Closers – are ready for this response and here is where they earn their reputation and commissions.

Here's the scenario again. The customer likes your presentation and proposal.

Summarize and Confirm that you have met their needs and buying criteria by repeating back to them what they told you was important

"You said your solution needed to have A, B, C. Check, check, check. So this product/service meets all those criteria, right?"

Ask for the Sale – very straightforward:

"I'd like to go ahead and get this written up (or get started, or get this rolling). Does that sound like a plan?"

"No. As I said, we are not going to make this decision today."

You asked for the sale one time – and they said "no".

You must be 100% prepared for this response. You should be expecting this every time. It should never come as a surprise.

Most salespeople say: *"Sure. I understand. When would you like me to follow up with you? Would 30 days from now be good?"*

Here's the Big Boys proceed. They ask for the sale again – this time using a "what if" question.

"I know you said that the timing is not right, but what if we could make a compelling offer? Would that earn your business today?"

"What if" are very powerful words. Rather than addressing their hesitation and timeline straight on, we are giving them a gentle push from the side.

"I know your timing is not right, but what if....." *"Might that change your timing?"*

This is an important step for two reasons. First, it really is your obligation to ask for the sale again – rather than just give up. Second, it gives the customer the opportunity to say yes. They may want to move forward, and all they need is a gentle (psychological) push.

There are two possible answers:

"As we said, we are not ready to move forward today."

Or

"What do you mean by compelling?"

In which case, obviously, you're on your way to a possible sale.

Assume they answered "no" again.

You have asked for the sale twice, and they said "no".

Here is your third close attempt.

"I can respect your decision process. You want to have all the facts before making a decision. That makes sense. But let

me ask - *you like the solution, it meets all your needs (criteria, wants, has all the features you want, etc.), and it was really what you were hoping to find, right?*

So in your mind, what issues are standing in the way of making this decision right now?"

With this specific word track, you have moved the focus off their decision not to proceed, and on to the reasons for that decision. You have also told them that the reasons for not moving forward are **in their mind**. They could, just as easily, move forward.

Here will be their answers:

> Think it over. Price. Do more research / Gather more information. Look at other options. Shop around. Not ready. Staying with our current solution, etc.

Get them to give you something <u>specific</u>.

Have them expand on their answer.

"What specifically do you mean when you say.....?"

"Tell me more about your research process."

"I certainly understand. You want to be 100% comfortable. It's an important decision. Obviously, there are some things with this solution that you're not comfortable with. Would you mind sharing them with me?"

Get them to give you the REASON for delaying their decision.

Isolate the issue:

"Besides _____, is there anything else that is preventing you from moving forward today?"

Get their commitment that this is the only issue, and if we can get that issue resolved, we can move forward.

"You need to do more research, but if the research checks out, can you see yourself using this?"

"So the price is not in line with what you were expecting, but if we can get the price to a point that makes sense, you would move forward with this, right?"

"So you would need more detail about the warranty and the processing of service claims, but if that checks out, then this would be the right fit and we could start today, right?"

Now you are in problem solving mode.

Use the two most powerful words in sales.

What if..............

> *we can get this to a price that makes sense?*
> *we can make this contingent on ....?*
> *we can start on a 3-month or 6-month trial basis?*
> *I can get a conference call set up with our CEO, so you get a sense of our company and how we operate?*
> *I can get that warranty extended another year?*
> *we can get the payments down to....?*
> *we are able to _____?*
>
> *Would that make a difference?*
> *I don't know if I can, but I'll try. Let me make a phone call / talk to my manager / pull something up in my system / etc.*

Great news. I think we can move forward. I was able to...

What if They Still Waffle?

You're still going to have people who waffle and waiver, afraid to commit, insistent on researching for another year about the best, the cheapest, etc. When a customer displays this behavior at this point, then you know they have a psychological problem making a decision, and a push is needed to help them with their problem.

At this point, you tell the customer what to do.

I'm still not sure.

It's a big commitment.

I'd feel better if we waited until...

I'm not ready to pull the trigger just yet.

You're right. Somewhere out there is the Holy Grail, but all that time, effort and expense you're going to spend looking for that perfect solution which may or may not exist, is wasted because you're overlooking this solution right here in front of us. Let's go ahead and get started. I promise you'll feel great when it's all settled.

It's a lot of money.

You're right. It is a lot of money. That's why we have been so careful in creating this proposal to exactly meet your needs. Let's go ahead and get started. I promise you'll feel great when it's all settled.

The Psychological Pin Down

As more sales move to the telephone, or even email exchanges, the technique of the psychological pin down has become more important.

When a customer says something like:

I'm just getting pricing right now. We will be moving forward in a few months.

Or

I need to get pricing from a few other sources.

This presents a problem because they might be getting a quote from you, and then shopping your quote around to several other suppliers.

They may or may not buy from you in the future. They may or may not be committed to you.

He might be saying this because he is just getting a ballpark price right now and the real project is a few months down the road, or he might be pricing you against others in the market.

When you have a longstanding relationship with a customer and they tell you they are just doing some preliminary pricing, you (should) have confidence that they will be coming back to you when they are ready to go.

However, if you do not have a relationship, they may or may not call you in a few months, or they may try to engage you in a price war with your competitor.

Use a pin-down statement to get them to commit to you.

"So when you pull the trigger on this project, you're going to call me right?"

"So you're going to buy that _____ from me, right?"

"Are you shopping this around right now?"

"How are we looking?"

"If you do get multiple quotes, you will give me the last look, right?"

Or... *"If you do get multiple quotes, will you give me the last look?"*

"When are you pulling the trigger on this? I will call you back, ok?"

Of course, the psychological pin down does not legally obligate the customer to call you back – some will, some won't - but by pinning them down, they are more likely to do so. Furthermore, once you have pinned the customer down, you can call back in a few weeks (or whatever appropriate timeframe) and you are now his buddy and you have a chance to share some additional information or insight or expertise. And the more friendly the conversation, the more likely he will come back to you when he's ready. You can even call him back the next day with some "news" about something, and keep building the relationship. The better the relationship, the more confident you can be that they will call you back.

Closing Techniques

Three Closes Are All You Will Ever Need

More sales books have been written about closing than about any other topic, and with good reason because most salespeople hesitate to close, or hesitate to put any pressure on a customer.

> **Closing is simply a statement or a series of statements that moves the conversation to the final step (payment / schedule / contract).**

Closing would be easy if you had a longstanding friendly relationship with the person.

> *"Hey are we going to talk all day, or are you going to take the credit card out of your wallet?"*

> *"You realize I don't get paid until you sign this, right?"*

> *"Are you going to make me sweat or are you going to give me the PO number?"*

> *"Hey you buy all your hardware from me, when are you going to start buying your software from me too?"*

If you are good friends with a customer, then that's exactly what you say to them. Or word it however you're comfortable. They have bought from you time and time again, and they will buy from you this time, and again in the future. You got this. You've got the inside track. This guy likes you, you like him, you provide him with a great product and great service at a fair price. The sales process gets compressed into *what do you need today? OK how are you paying?*

The point is, if you have a repeat relationship – closing is simple.

However, if this is your first transaction, you need to work for it.

Closing comes after all the steps in the process. The outdated concepts of ABC (Always Be Closing) and the hard close or the gimmick close has been long debunked and disproven. People need to go through the full psychological process of learning and becoming comfortable with you and the solution. They have to understand the solution, and feel it is a good fit for them.

These are the steps of the sales process you need to walk through with each prospective customer.

- Cold Call
- Warm Call
- Green Light Statements (yes we can – you've come to the right place – I know exactly what you're talking about)
- Relationship Statements
- Needs Development
- Listening (questions, reflecting, paraphrasing, probe & clarify)
- Presentation (based on everything you have told me, this is what I think will work best)
- Trial Close (How does this sound so far?)
- Dealing with Questions, Concerns and Objections (Be prepared. Agree and ask additional questions. When you have identified the real objection, you can read your responses right off your Battle Cards – nobody is going to ask you a question or give you an objection you haven't already heard a hundred times – be prepared)

- Trial Close (Sound reasonable? Yes that sounds good.)
- Now it already is closed – we need to move to the next step (payment/schedule/contract).

Start with these three closes. All three assume we are moving ahead.

Is there anything we haven't addressed?

Do you have any more questions?

Then the customer says: *No. I think you've answered all my questions.*

- **Assumptive Close (you assume the sale is over)**

    "I really appreciate your business. Thanks."

    "I just need a credit card to get this rolling."

    "Let's give this a try and see how it goes."

    "Let's get this rolling."

    "What other projects do you have coming up after this one? Let's get this order delivered, then we can get into more detail on that other project."

    "I can have this delivered by Thursday, would that be good for you?"

    "I can have the agreement written up by the end of the day tomorrow. We'll meet Friday 9am at the lawyer's office downtown to sign off, ok?"

    "Let me get the credit card first, then I want to verify the shipping address."

    "We can schedule the kickoff meeting for Monday, can you make that work for your team?"

    "If I had my installer come on Tuesday morning, how's that going to fit with the rest of the work you have going on?"

"I'm finishing up another project today and tomorrow, but we should be able to start Tuesday afternoon, how does that work? Will someone be there to let us in?"

"Which credit card do you have for me?"

"Do you want to apply for Net 30 payment or are you going to use a credit card for this?"

"I want to go ahead and start pulling the project team together – are you going to make that first payment in cash or write me a check?"

"I'm going to schedule this for Tuesday. Will someone be here around 9am?"

- **A or B Choice Close – Close by giving the customer a choice**

    "We talked about upgrading the user license, did you want to do that or stay with the standard license for now?"
    "Do you need this contract to be in the company name, or in your personal name?"
    "Will this be written up for you alone, or for you and your wife jointly?"
    "Did you want to extend the warranty to five years, or are you staying with the standard three year warranty?"
    "It will take me about two days to get the materials together, do you want me to start Thursday, or will next Monday be better?"
    "Do you want to give me a credit card to get this rolling, or are you going to apply for Net 30 payment terms with us and then we can send you an invoice?"

- **The List Close**

    "OK each of the owners will receive a cash payment of $1.6M plus 2,300,000 preferred shares. The existing *facility will remain open, and all key employees will be given a guaranteed two year employment agreement plus stock options based on their seniority and level of service. Does that cover everything we discussed? What else do we need to include in the contract?"*

"OK you said you wanted the 32GB RAM, the 1TB hard drives, the mid-range CPU? Delivery late next week. What else?"

"OK you said you wanted the one time termite treatment, then the weekly pest control service with the standard warranty. What else?"

"OK I'm going to list this house with the washer/dryer included, you are leaving all the window treatments, you have a lifetime termite certification, you will repair the garage door. What else do we need to specify when we list the home?"

You shouldn't need any tricks or gimmicks to guide the conversation to the close (payment / schedule / contract). It's a process built on asking good questions and listening, being prepared and expert at dealing with questions and concerns, then moving the conversation to a tie-down and the close.

One More Closing Technique:

"Here's What's Going to Happen Next."

Here's one more simple and effective close that moves the conversation from questions to taking action.

As always:

"What other questions do you have?"

Or

"Do you have any other questions?"

"No. I think that's it."

Or

"Have we cleared that up?"

"Yes we have."

OK Great.

Here's What's Going to Happen Next

Or

Here's What We Do Next

"You're going to pull your car around back…"

   "I'm going to introduce you to your project manager and he/she will review your…"

   "I'm going to submit this form, and tomorrow you will get a call from…"

   "You will finalize the color choice, and …."

"You're going to pick a delivery date and..."

"We will get started on the design immediately and then....."

"After we do the paperwork, ..."

"We will start the build process and you should get a completion date by...."

Simply describe the process moving forward.

Now get the signature, or credit card, or whatever is required to seal the deal.

It would be common for more questions to pop up at this point, but you can simply answer them and ask for the signature, credit card, etc. after your answer.

Creating Urgency

How Can We Get Them to Buy Today?

It's the age old question in sales. The customer likes our product, but they want to wait to make a decision. So how do we get a customer to act now, to buy now, to sign now - rather than put it off another day, another month, another year?

Every salesperson knows the odds of closing go way down if the sale is not closed today. They promise they will be back, but they very rarely come back. Even if they intend to come back, circumstances change, they get new information, our competitors find them.

In general, people are uncomfortable making a decision, or making a new commitment. There is a tendency to leave things the way they are. Psychologically speaking, it's more comfortable to keep the status quo.

As salespeople we want to find ways to create urgency, to give them a reason to act today.

The problem with creating urgency is that anyone over the age of 10 is not fooled by *"this sale ends today"* or *"this price is only good for today"*. They know that "urgency" is a gimmick that has been over-used by retail stores and salespeople forever. They know that if they don't buy it today, they can buy it tomorrow, or next week, or next month, or next year. They realize that if they miss this Once in a Lifetime Sale, there will be another Once in a Lifetime Sale next week.

"It's the only one left" no longer has an effect on customers. They can go on the internet and find a hundred more just like it,

or a hundred other companies who can offer the same product or service.

Here are a few different ways you can incorporate urgency into your sales process.

There are two types of urgency.

1. Situational Urgency

There is a problem with the current situation.

Business as usual is no longer viable.

The current situation is no longer acceptable.

Every day the customer delays results in loss or suffering.

From time to time, you will find a customer who recognizes the urgency of their situation and starts the sales call by telling you they need to buy something today.

However, the more common situation is that your customer is in no rush. They are gathering information, they are researching, or they are just looking and planning on buying in the future.

The technique to create urgency is to ask **Anxiety Questions** as part of your Needs Development.

Once you understand what their problem is - why they are talking to you in the first place - you simply ask them what would happen if they don't take action now to solve the problem. Don't tell them they have to take action now, lead them to it through questioning.

Here's an example of a customer who recognizes the urgency in their situation.

In a florist shop, the cooling mechanism in the refrigerator is not working. Of course, if they don't get the refrigerator fixed immediately, they will lose their flower inventory and lose money.

So when they call a refrigerator repair company, they tell them they need the refrigerator repaired today:

"Do you have the right part, and how fast can you get here?"

Of course, most of us are not that lucky, so let's change this scenario to a florist who is shopping for a new refrigerator. Right now, they are just doing some research on different models and different prices. They are planning on buying in six to nine months.

You're going to start out by asking Needs Development questions.

"OK great. Let me show you a few different Florist Refrigeration units. Before I tell you about the refrigeration units we carry can you tell me a little about the unit you have now. What size is it? Do you know the BTU rating of your current unit? What do you like about it? What don't you like about it? How long have you had it? What research have you done so far on new refrigerator units? What is your timeframe to replace your existing unit?" etc.

Add Anxiety Questions as part of your Needs Development process.

"So your current unit is 12 years old. Fast forward a few months from now... What would happen if it failed? What would your losses be? What if it failed on a day when your store is closed? What would happen if it was a total loss?"

You are allowing the customer to tell you the risks and negative consequences of not moving forward.

You are drawing their attention to the worst case risk scenario. You are creating FUD – Fear, Uncertainty, and Doubt.

Then you come to the (psychological) rescue.

"I understand. Our company has helped hundreds of florists in your exact situation. We guarantee four-hour installation, and once installed, our units self-monitor the compressors, so if the unit stops

working - even for a few seconds - you and our service department will be alerted to the failure and we'll have someone on-site within an hour with the parts needed to fix it."

"Now let me show you a few refrigeration units that I think will meet your needs."

Or if you're selling life insurance and the couple says *"We can't afford it just yet – maybe in about six months this will make more sense."*

Anxiety Question:

"Let's fast forward six months and suppose something happened to you. What would happen to your family if you didn't have this insurance?"

In these examples, we're not telling the customer they have to act now. We are helping to uncover and point out to them the risks of not moving forward. We are allowing them to discover Situational Urgency, that business as usual is not good enough.

Create Situational Urgency by asking Anxiety Questions to help them see the risk.

2. Emotional Urgency

All buying decisions have two components - an emotional decision, followed by a logical analysis of the cost/benefits or price/value proposition. If the logical analysis supports the emotional decision, they move forward.

Emotional urgency is designed to encourage a customer to take action right now - based on the emotion - before the logical mind begins its analysis.

Red Tag Special Pricing

Black Friday Specials

Scarcity

Exclusivity

Pride

Fear

Fear of missing out

Greed

Love

Sex

Today only

Regret

Pity

Shame

Using Fear to Create Urgency

Here's an example of how a lawyer would use fear to create urgency.

You open your mail and you see a legal summons requiring you to appear in court on a certain day. You research the best lawyers for this type of legal work and call the first lawyer.

"It's very important that you respond to that summons immediately, and in the correct way. If you respond incorrectly or delay at all, you could potentially lose your rights and could be exposed to further legal complications down the road."

At this point you are afraid to handle this yourself. You could lose your rights AND be exposed to further legal complications. That sounds awful.

"Do you have the summons in front of you? Great. Go ahead and fax it to me. I'll transfer you to my administrative assistant who will give you the fax number and take your credit card information so we can get our response prepared quickly."

To enhance the effectiveness of the emotional appeal, make the transaction as quick and easy as possible so it can be

completed in the grip of the emotion – right now - before the logical mind has time to get involved. Because the logical mind will always find reasons why the purchase should not be made, or why more research is necessary.

In this case, if the transaction is not completed immediately, the customer will make the logical decision to do more research, and perhaps contact more lawyers who can handle this and choose a lawyer who may offer a lower price, or may even decide to handle the matter himself.

Using Fear of Missing Out (FOMO) to Create Urgency

A retail salesperson wearing a simple sticker generates a fear of missing out:

Ask me about our June Specials

What does every customer do when they see that sticker?

"Tell me about your specials"

"Well, you said you had a longer time horizon on this purchase, so I didn't think you would be interested. These specials only apply to items sold and delivered this month, so we will need to act quickly to get the special price."

Then on July 1st:

Ask me about our July Specials

Most TV commercials are targeted to emotional appeal. Websites will have countdown clocks, or show "Limited Quantity" or "Only one unit left! Act now!"

Emotional urgency is most effective if the customer has a strong desire for the product. It is much less effective if the customer is not convinced of the need for the product.

"If you like it, you really should get it now. It's the last one in stock, and I'd hate for you to lose it."

Your job is to think about your sales process and invent ways to create urgency.

Using a Time Limit to Create Urgency

"I wanted to let you know that we're raising our prices effective July 1st, so we are giving our existing customers 60 days notice. Any orders received on or before June 30th will be at the current prices."

Using a Time Limit and a Value Bump to Create Urgency

"To encourage new customers to sign up this month, we are bumping them up to the Gold benefits package (at no extra charge), and locking in this year's pricing for the next three years. Guaranteed."

Using Limited Availability and the Fear of Losing to Create Urgency

"Whoever places the order first is going to get it. I don't know when it will be sold, but once it is sold, the opportunity is gone."

"I don't know how long our inventory on this unit is going to last. Obviously, if you know you are going to buy it anyway, then it would make sense to do it sooner rather than later, don't you think?"

Using Exclusivity to Create Urgency

"When we launch we are only going to allow five Beta Customers. Those customers are going to receive one on one support, and lock in the Beta pricing for the next three years."

"We only have room for three featured businesses on our home page."

Using Pride and Prestige to Create Urgency

"This is the premier charity event in the city. We appreciate you and your wife attending last year, but I was hoping this year you could sponsor a table, and will consider being one of our primary sponsors. You and your business will be highlighted, and as a

premier sponsor, you will have three minutes to speak and to present one of the awards for the evening."

Using Greed to Create Urgency

"This company is expecting approval of its patent any day, and when that happens the stock could sky rocket. This could be the next IBM. And when you read about it in the Wall Street Journal, it will be too late. The time to get in is NOW while the stock is still trading for under $1."

Submitting a Bid or Proposal

Last is Best

Job interviews, proposals, and figure skating – all other things being equal – last is best.

Primacy and Recency

The psychological principle of Primacy says that we remember the beginning of a process or presentation. Recency says we remember the last thing we see.

A figure skating judge will almost never give the first competitor a 10 – no matter how great they are – because they have to see all the contestants before they can decide if the first one is really worthy of a 10. Unfortunately the judges never go back and revise their scores for the first person.

It's the same if you are the first person to interview for a job. You may be awesome, but they have to reserve their enthusiasm (their final judgment) until they see all the other candidates because there may be someone better. If you are the last candidate and you sweep them away, they can allow themselves to get swept away because they've already seen everyone else. They are in a position now to make a final judgment.

On a job interview, if you find that you are scheduled for the first interview or one of the first interviews – find an excuse to push your interview back one week. They will not make a decision without interviewing all the candidates, and you have a much better chance of making a lasting impression if you are last (that's why it's called a "lasting" impression).

Now obviously you need to be a very strong candidate and be totally prepared for the interview, there's no substitute for being the best candidate, but if you are early in the process it's easy for you to get lost in the crowd, even if you were the best candidate. That's just the psychological truth.

It's the same when submitting a proposal or bid. Always be the last to submit. Only the last bid can lock up the deal right there on the spot. They can't get too excited about the first proposal because they haven't seen the other proposals, but if you're last you can close the deal right there because they already have all the facts.

If they like you they will usually be more than willing to share the details of the other proposals so you can see exactly what they quoted and how they arrived at their price. Even if your price is higher you should be able to justify by explaining to the customer all the details that he said was important. If you have knowledge of the competing bids you can also point out the materials they specified, their labor rate, etc., and use all that information to your advantage.

The advantages of going last seem obvious. Imagine you are a Real Estate Agent and you are working with a couple who has been trying to sell the house themselves – now they are interviewing three agents to decide who will list their home.

If you go first and tell them the house should list at $270,000 – you have no shot if someone comes after you and tells them their house is worth $310,000. If you're last you can see what the other agents have told them. You can gather all that information and show them and prove to them that you're the best. If you ask questions, listen and gather all the competing information, trial close, then move toward the close – I can't imagine how you could lose!

Proposal Strategy When You Are Not the Lowest Price

One other important point about creating a bid or a proposal. When you are the lowest price you want all the bids to be identical. You are obviously in the best position to win.

When you are not the lowest price, you want to propose something different or unique. If your proposal is identical, then you will lose. If you shake it up and twist it around and show them a variety of possibilities, it becomes difficult for them to compare apples to apples. Have them choose which of your different proposals they like best.

Putting it All Together With an Example:

A carpenter creating a proposal for a home improvement project

Of course carpenters don't think of themselves as salespeople, but imagine how many more projects they could work on (how much more money they could make / how many more people they could employ) if they would take the initiative to learn the sales process?

You have scheduled an appointment to meet with the homeowner to review his home improvement project and create your bid proposal.

You want to be last. Do everything you can within reason to be the last contractor to visit the site and prepare a bid.

What if you can't be last?

If you can't be the last bid then say: *"I will get this proposal ready for you and after you have received all the other bids I would like to meet with you again to review and compare, ok?" Thank you. I really appreciate that.* (psychological pindown)

Now let's say you have scheduled yourself as the last contractor to bid.

Ask Needs Development Questions and gather competitive information:

"Let's take a look at the project."
"What did you have in mind?"

> *"What are you trying to accomplish?"*
> *"What is most important to you?"*
> *"What materials were you thinking of using?"*
> *"How did the other contractors handle this?"*
> *"We can do that with a cheaper plastic configuration or a higher quality metal piece – in general, how important is quality to you on this project?"*
> *"What materials did the other contractors use?"*
> *"How many hours did they estimate?"*
> *"Do we have to deal with any zoning regulations?"*
> *"When did you want to have this project completed?"* (Oh! We better get this started!)
> *"Did the other contractors quote you 50% up front, 50% on completion?"*
> *Etc.*

If you ask great questions you are already ahead of 99% of contractors who simply don't take the time to find out what's on the customer's mind. The customer will feel comfortable with you because you are taking the time to ask questions and get into the details, then you are feeding back the issues that are important to them. They know (and they're right) that you will take the time to fully understand their ideas and preferences.

Reflect and paraphrase:

> *Oh so you want dark wood trim around the skylight?*
> *Oh so you want people to be able to open this door and have access to the counter from this direction?*

Remember, you are reflecting and paraphrasing for two reasons. First, the customer will volunteer more information which will allow you to ask more questions and understand their needs better. Second is to make the customer feel listened to – to help them realize that you, and you alone, have taken the time to really understand this project.

Trial Close - See where you stand:

"How does this look?"
"What do you think?"
"What questions do you have for me?"
"This would look great, don't you think?"
"Any concerns or additions before we finalize?"

Be 100% prepared for all the common objections:

The other guys are cheaper.

"I understand. You're looking for the best price."

Now ask a question: "Let's find out if the less expensive proposal is a true apples to apples comparison."

Go back and re-explain the difference in materials, or the extra things that you are going to do – which he told you are important to him. Just one example, you mentioned you wanted that dark wood trim on the skylight – I'm sure these other bids don't have that same level of detail. When this is done, all the details are going to be exactly the way you want them, you know?

I need to see your references.

Shame on you. You should have brought your photo portfolio with you. This objection should have been taken care of during your presentation.

I'm not sure I can afford this project, all the bids were more than I had budgeted.

"I understand, everyone has to work within a budget. There are several ways we can cut down the scope of the project to either reduce materials or labor."

"What specifically would you like to cut out so we can get to your budget?"

Or you can use a Loss Statement to get him to feel comfortable with the over-budget price.

"I understand, this is a big project. You have a lot of really cool features in this design and your house is going to look great. These upgrades make the house much more valuable. It's a great investment, don't you think? And you will enjoy your house much more every day, you know? We absolutely can cut the budget, but then you would be losing...."

The Close – Here are Some Examples for This Home Contractor

Review these closing statements/questions and create similar statements that relate to your situation.

Assume that you have already won (Assumptive Close):

"I can have the materials together by Monday, would that be a good day to start?"

"We should be able to start next week, you know?"

"I'm finishing up another project today and tomorrow, but we should be able to start Tuesday afternoon, how does that work?"

"Do you want to cut the first check now or do you want to give us the check when we start next week?"

Or... *"I want to go ahead and start pulling the materials together – are you going to make that first payment in cash or write me a check?"*

"I'm going to go ahead and schedule this for Tuesday. Will someone be here around 9am?"

Close by Giving the Customer a Choice (A or B Close):

"We talked about adding that second skylight, did you want to do that or stay with just the one?"

"We talked about extending the cabinets another 12", did you want to stay with the original length or add that extra foot?"

"It will take me about two days to get all the materials together, do you want me to start Thursday, or will next Monday work better for you?"

"Do you want to cut the first check now or do you want to give us the check when we start next week?"

Review the Details and Close the Deal (Shopping List Close):

"OK so let's see – we had the skylight with the dark wood trim, the upgraded countertop, the etc. etc."

Customer says Yes, yes, yes, yes, yes. *"Is there anything else we need to include?"*

Then: *"OK let's get this scheduled right now. What start date works best for you?"*

Cold Calling

Let's think about this. If you've gotten this far in the book it's a good bet that you are at least a good salesperson. You've got skills and you're working on improving those skills. If I was the sales manager and I got a really important lead and I needed to give it to someone that I had confidence would do a good job with this lead – you're probably the one I'd give it to because I know you're going to do your best to work it and build a relationship with the customer.

Now if you're good, and you don't consistently cold call – then imagine the results you would get if you did consistently cold call for targeted high end opportunities. You're working on raising your game every day by being aware of your sales skills and working on adding new skills and refining.

Now let's raise your game another notch and get you to cold call the big opportunities.

Cold Calling is defined as calling on someone who does not know you, and is not expecting your call.

In this day and age of voicemail, it is quite difficult to reach a target customer. In fact, if the customer is high value and worth reaching (buyer, CIO, HR Director, Wealthy Individual, etc.) you can be sure that everyone is trying to reach them, and they are bombarded by phone calls.

So the best advice when cold calling is to either call a list of people who are easy to reach (easier to reach, but lower value targets), or create a "dream list" of 50 accounts and try to reach the key contact in each of those accounts (harder to reach, but higher value).

When you cold call, you get more "at bats", more proposals in your pipeline, more opportunities with large potential accounts. Salespeople who are good at cold calling are busier and make more money than salespeople who wait for the phone to ring. It's really that simple.

Salespeople who avoid cold calling, or who are not good at cold calling, or have a poor work ethic in general, simply don't make as much money as salespeople who make it a habit to cold call every day and then work to improve their cold calling success rate.

Here's what you need to do today.

1. Choose a different attitude about cold calling (a different set of facts)
2. Set realistic goals for your cold calling activity
3. Use a step by step approach on every call

> Suppose at your next sales meeting your sales manager hands each salesperson five index cards, each with the name of a Fortune 100 company. In addition to the commissions you may earn over the next several years from landing such a large account, the sales manager is going to give $1,000 to the first person who gets an order of any size from any of the accounts on the list. The offer expires in 90 days.

What would you do first?

You would try to locate anyone in that company who will take the time to listen to you and help you navigate the company. You might go to Facebook or LinkedIn, you might go to chat rooms, you might dial the main switchboard, you might call a company that sells non-competing products into those accounts – they might be able to guide you who to talk to.

Before you call anyone on your dream list, do your research. Check on social marketing sites like Linkedin to see if you can locate the name(s) of people in your target area.

The vast majority of time spent in cold calling, and the most unpleasant part of cold calling is working your way through different people in an organization to find someone who will listen and help. Nobody is going to return your call, and if you do actually talk to someone they may give you a hard roadblock and not help. Others will direct you to someone else, while still others will direct you back to the main company number and tell you to "just ask for purchasing." "Ok I'll do that. Thank you soooo much!"

Use the plan and the example below and try this for yourself. Identify five big potential new customers, put the names of the companies on index cards, and go. See what happens.

Raise your game.

Give yourself five index cards once a month.

Cold Calling

Adjust Your Attitude

I'm sure it would not surprise you that if you survey any group of salespeople they will say

Cold Calling is:

    A waste of time

    A horrible experience

    A low percentage activity

    Useless

    Unpleasant

    Painful

    Pointless

    Can't get past the gatekeeper

    Not for me

    Worked for me once, but have never had any good results since

   While cold calling may be all these things, it is the life blood of many salespeople, and can be a great way to pick up large new accounts. So we need to adjust our attitude about cold calling and turn it into a positive.

   You can choose to think of cold calling in a negative light, **or you can choose to think of cold calling in a different way**.

Cold Calling is:

Like a box of chocolates - you never know what you're going to get

A way to continue improving your sales skills

Gold Calling

Interesting

Beneficial to your new clients

Providing new information to them

Definitely worth your time

Respectful

Thought provoking

A learning experience for you

Honest communication

A necessary responsibility to those who depend on you to be great

A professional activity

A way to expand your account base and make more money

Take your five index cards, take your positive attitude and start calling.

Cold Calling

Realistic Goals for the Cold Call

The main goal in the cold call process is to navigate the company and make contact with a knowledgeable person, and engage in at least a small sales platform.

In cold calling, by far the most time consuming and most unpleasant activity is navigating the company to find someone who will talk to you and has an understanding of your product or service.

If you are talking to yet another person who is not the 'decision maker', all is not lost. Of course, you will ask for their help guiding you to the decision maker, but you should also gather information about the company and their needs.

Once you are engaged in a conversation with a knowledgeable person – that should be fun! You're a salesperson, so you should enjoy this type of conversation and you should enjoy the opportunity to flex your sales skills.

The second goal in the cold calling process is to turn this initial conversation into a warm call.

The purpose in speaking to a new prospect is to share with them that your company is another option, an alternative to doing what they are currently doing, an alternative to their current method or solution, an alternative to their current vendor.

Once you have engaged in even a small sales conversation, this account is now just like all your other accounts. You're done cold calling. You have succeeded. You have a contact, you have notes from your conversation, and you have a reason to call back, even if it's just to "check in".

You can hope, and it does happen occasionally, but it would be unreasonable to expect that a brand new contact is going to hand all his business to you on the first call. Your experience will fall into one of the following categories:

- There is no need for your product or service. You thought there would be, but for one reason or another, you find out there is no need.
- There is a need, but they already are firmly entrenched with a competitor or a different way to accomplish the same thing without your product or service. They are simply not open to you as an alternative.
- There is a need, but the decision is made elsewhere. Maybe they have outsourced those decisions to a third party company, or they are a subsidiary company and all decisions are made at corporate headquarters.
- There is a need, but they have just made a large purchase with a competitor, or invested in a different way to accomplish the task.
- There is a need, but it is a year or two away.
- There is a need and they are willing to test you with a small item to see if you can deliver on what you said.

Once you have arrived at one of the above results, this is no longer a cold call. This account is now just like every other account you're working. You have a contact, you have notes, you have a follow up call scheduled, or you have marked this account as a non-prospect.

When you engage in the initial sales conversation:

- If he is receptive, then simply begin your needs development questions.

- If it's not a fit, thank him for his time, hang up the phone, and send him your contact information and brochure in an email and ask him if he would be kind enough to forward your information to anyone who might need it, "as a professional favor to help grow my professional network."

- If it's a future opportunity, then put him on your two or three month follow up. When you follow up you have an opportunity to assume he is familiar with you, and just start talking like you're old friends. "I know you don't have anything right now, but I hope you don't mind these follow up calls every few months just to check in." Of course they don't mind. "Now if anything comes up before then, you're going to give me a call right?" "I'm your guy. I'll make sure we take good care of you."

When customers don't want your products or services, it is very important to understand why they don't need it, or why they are happy with a competitor, or are just not interested. The more you know why customers don't buy your product, the wider and broader will be your understanding of your industry. This will give you a better perspective as you talk to more customers.

Cold Calling

A Step by Step Plan

Every time I pick up the phone it's my expectation that these new customers actually need my products and services, and would be happy to find out that they have another option. I understand in advance that even when they are receptive, the timing may not be now. We may have just missed an opportunity, or they may be months or years away from being ready.

Step 1:   Research and choose the best customers with the most likely payoff

Step 2:   Ask for help locating the right person

Step 2a: If not the right person, use them to gather information

Step 2b: If you get a putoff, memorize your putoff responses

Step 3:   If they are the right person – Give a quick introduction of you and your company

Step 4:   A brief statement of benefit targeted to what you already know about them

Step 5:   Ask an Implied Question

Step 6:   If you get an open response - move into your needs development and treat this like a regular sales call

Step 6a: If you get a putoff, memorize your putoff responses.

Cold Calling

Leaving a Voice Message

When you get to the actual decision maker, or the correct buyer in a big corporation, or if you're targeting individuals such as high wealth individuals, or top real estate agents, or top doctors, etc., you need to understand that for the very reason these people are worth calling, they are bombarded by salespeople on a daily basis.

The percentage of calls that go to voice mail is now approaching 90%. More than half of those messages are NOT RETURNED.

In reality, people do return calls when they get a voice message:

From their spouse, their doctor, their lawyer, their insurance company, their accountant, their customers, their boss, their friends and relatives, their children's school, etc.

They just don't return your calls.

Why don't they return your calls? Because you are a salesperson.

How do they know you're a salesperson?

1. You talk about your company and your product
2. You talk about how much you can help them
3. You talk fast and sound eager
4. You give them too much information in the message

The Big Book of Sales

    5. You repeat your phone number twice (only salespeople do that)

You have had salespeople call you, and you can immediately spot the difference between an important call and a sales call. You immediately resist and tell them you're not interested. If they leave a message, you don't call them back.

The reality is that people don't want sales calls, and as salespeople continue to bombard business people, many have developed the habit of not taking any calls, but simply go through voice messages and jot down the number, or delete.

Develop a four step approach to try to reach your target.

    1. Leave a brief message.

Your TONE is key. Slow, authoritative, do not sound excited, do not raise your inflection at the end of the sentence. Speak as if you were an attorney leaving a message for your client.

"Alan Gordon at ABC Industries 212-123-4567. I'll be in the office until 4:30 today. Please call me."

Even with that, you probably won't get a call back.

    2. Wait 3-4 days.

Leave another brief message.

"This is Alan Gordon at ABC Industries calling again. 212-123-4567. I would appreciate a return call. Thank you."

    3. Wait 3-4 days. This time we are going to offer some knowledge and expertise.

"This is Alan Gordon at ABC Industries again. I wanted to bring you up to speed on several important changes in _____ that apply to you (your business/your company/your etc.), and make sure that you are aware of these changes. Please call me. I will be in the office until 4:30 today. 212-123-4567."

4. Wait 3-4 days. This time we are going to repeat the offer, tell them this is the last contact, and use a <u>loss statement</u>.

"This is Alan Gordon at ABC Industries again. I don't want to continue to bother you so I'm not going to call again, but I did want to bring you up to speed on several important changes in _____ that pertains directly to you. You are free to call me or not call me, but I would hate for you to not get this information. I would appreciate a return call at 212-123-4567. Thank you."

Beyond this, put a reminder to call in three months. In general, work with people who want to work with you. Some people recommend calling every day, even every hour. Some people recommend leaving trick messages, or leaving a message that you are angry at them or disappointed with them. All in all, it is my opinion that I want to work with people who want to work with me. And I will call back in a month or two and start the cycle again.

If and when they do call you back, or answer the phone you are now buddies. They will remember your name and the series of messages you left. They know your voice, they have heard your authoritative and relaxed personality in your messages, they appreciate your persistence, they know you're an expert, and as long as you recognize that their time is valuable, they will speak to you as a professional. They are now giving you a shot.

"Susan! Great to hear from you."

"Let me share with you what's going on here."

Then go into your opening statement – which of course, should be scripted until you have it memorized. Your opening statement should lead quickly into Needs Development.

Here are some other words of advice in a first conversation:

- When calling corporate cultures, use words like "metrics and measuring"
- We provide another option
- Be amiable, honest, respectful, to the point, and listen to his responses.
- Paint a future picture of successful results
- Show knowledge of their market and others in their industry you have worked with
- Include a next step
- Avoid self-undermining statements such as:

    You probably never heard of our company

    You probably don't know me

    You may not be interested, but

    I know you're really busy, but

    You may not be the right person to speak to, but

    We currently don't do business, but

Remember, you're typically not selling anything on a first contact. All you're doing is making him aware of another option and identifying his current state of need.

As a general rule, I like doing business with people who want to do business with me. While it is certainly true that a year or more after leaving a series of messages, a client has called me back and done business with me, in general I like to move on to more receptive people. But there are situations where there may only be 5 or 10 potential customers, and you need to be persistent.

Cold Calling

Crafting a Concise Opening Statement

When you reach your target on the phone you must have a very concise opening statement.

The purpose of your opening statement is to frame the conversation, then immediately roll into Needs Development questions.

"Hi Jack/Susan/Dr. Bennett/Mr. Welsh, this is Alan Gordon at ABC Industries."

"Did I catch you at a bad time?" (impulsive opposition)

To which they will almost always answer "No, I have a minute what's this about?"

Next will be a very brief benefit statement – you're going to identify one or two benefits that you bring to companies like theirs, or people like them.

"We have been successful working with companies in the ____ industry, (now the benefit statement) saving them quite a bit of money, and allowing them to attract new customers." (or whatever your primary benefit statement is).

Offer information or education (tailor to your product or industry).

"I wanted to bring you up to speed on the changes that are taking place in our industry, and the new regulations that are going to have an effect on all of us."

Now, include an "objection cancellation" statement.

Here are two common objections that we all get.

I'm not interested

I already have a vendor / solution for that

So immediately after the benefit statement, we include an objection cancellation statement. When you acknowledge the objection yourself at the very beginning, you are proceeding with the understanding that they can no longer bring up that particular objection. I'm telling you up front that you should be interested – so you can't tell me later that you're not interested. I'm telling you up front that you already have another vendor for this – so you can't tell me later that you already have someone else – I already told you that.

"These changes are so important that every _____ should be interested."

"I know you already have a (solution/plan/vendor) for this, and I'm sure it's working quite well."

Now finally we ask a question – and this question should result in a NO

"Are you aware of all the new changes in _____?"

"No? Ok let me ask you…"

Then roll into your Needs Development questions.

Here's the whole process rolled into a concise opening. As you read through it, notice it takes about 30 seconds – which is the perfect time for an opening statement.

Your tone of voice is very important in your opening statement.

Slow and confident. When you start out slowly, it pulls them into listening to you.

Selling a Payroll/Benefits Package to a Director of HR.

Ring. Ring. Ring.

"Julie Phillips."

INTRODUCTION

"Hi Julie, I'm Alan Gordon at ABC Payroll Systems." (try to say this very slowly – your very first sentence will dictate the pace of the entire call – do you sound like you are interrupting them, or like you have valuable information for them?)

ASK FOR PERMISSION TO CONTINUE – USE IMPULSIVE OPPOSITION

" Did I catch you at a bad time?"

"No I have a minute, what's this about?"

BRIEF BENEFIT STATEMENT

"We work with many mid-size businesses such as yours to provide very creative and low-cost benefit plans, and our payroll systems are designed to take all the work off you, and save you time."

OFFER INFORMATION OR EDUCATION

"Technology is changing very rapidly in the Benefits industry, and I wanted to bring you up to speed on some of these changes."

OBJECTION BLOCKER

"I know you obviously already have a solution for Payroll and Benefits, but are you aware of all the recent changes that have been going on?"

"No."

IMMEDIATELY ROLL INTO NEEDS DEVELOPMENT

"OK. Let me ask you, what system are you currently using for Payroll and Benefits?" "How do you currently administer….?"

"Etc."

If you have an opportunity to inject personality or humor or some common bonding – by all means do so here in the beginning. However, this concise opening is designed to immediately roll you into a Needs Development conversation – which is where you want to be.

Cold Calling

Handling Control Statements

People have a natural impulse to resist a cold call. In my own experience, I will talk with people I don't know, but if I don't know you, and you are trying to sell me something I will stop the call as soon as possible.

This impulsive resistance is normal human nature. We do it to salespeople who call us, and our customers do it to us.

"Look. You can stop right there. I'm not interested."

"Who are you?"

"Are you trying to sell me something?"

"Are you a salesman?"

"How did you get my number?"

"Look. Can you please take me off your list."

*"If you're selling something I'm not intereste*d."

When we make these types of statements, we are not only displaying resistance, but more importantly we are asserting our control over the conversation. I'm not letting you speak any more. I'm done because I say I'm done. This conversation is over.

Your opening statement takes 15-30 seconds. When the customer throws out this type of a control statement in the first few seconds, they have quickly identified you as a salesperson and are telling you that you are intruding on them. THEY DO NOT WANT TO BE ENGAGED IN THIS CONVERSATION WITH YOU

– EVEN THOUGH THEY DON'T HAVE ANY IDEA ABOUT YOUR PRODUCT OR SERVICE OR PROGRAM.

These are very natural statements, but how do you handle them?

> "Look – are you selling something? Because we can end this call right now."

> "Jack/Susan/Dr. Smith/Mr. Thompson you sound like someone who doesn't want to waste time, and I'm the same way. Let's just take a second to see if we have a match, does that sound reasonable? What system are you currently using for Payroll/Benefits?"

We acknowledged the interruption.

We agreed with them. I don't want to waste your time either.

We guided them to take a brief moment to stay with the process.

We immediately went into Needs Development.

Cold Calling

Example

Let's analyze a cold call situation, and then learn how to improve your success rate.

CASE STUDY #1 – Commercial Air Conditioning Systems:

Background:

   Commercial Air Solutions sells rooftop air conditioning systems to large commercial buildings. They do an audit of your current system to rate efficiency, then show you a plan to install more energy efficient systems which will cut monthly electricity bills. It's a free audit, so you have nothing to lose. They can also guide you to available state or federal rebates when installing a more efficient system that uses less electricity. Typical results are a savings of 30% per month on your electric bill which normally results in a Return on Investment (ROI) of 10 months, with 30% savings on every electric bill beyond that.

   If you are planning new construction, or your current system is more than three years old, it's a no-brainer offer - but the problem is that when cold calling - even though the customer would benefit from the audit, they are rejecting the calls and simply aren't interested.

GOAL OF A COLD CALL:

The purpose of the cold call is to create a Sales Platform where you can ask questions to uncover facts, build a relationship, relate your solution to their situation, and schedule an energy audit. The cold call will result in a Sales Platform as brief as one minute, or if everything goes great, the call may last 15 or 20 minutes.

Needs Development Questions:

- *What air conditioning equipment do you have installed now?*
- *Do you know what year it was installed?*
- *How many years are left on the warranty?*
- *What is your monthly electric bill?*
- *When is the last time you conducted an energy audit?*
- *What type of Green initiatives do you have in place?*
- *Have you ever heard of pre-chilled air flow? No? This one technology alone is saving large facilities 30% on their electric bills.*
- *Do you know the last year your company took the State/Federal Energy Rebate? Never?*

INTRODUCTION:

Very quick introduction of you, your company, and what you do:

Hello John/Joan, I'm Alan Gordon with Commercial Air Solutions specializing in air conditioning systems and energy savings for buildings with more than 30,000 square feet. I'd like to take a minute to tell you about the changes in technology, and also what's going on with the new state Green Initiatives.

Use impulsive disagreement to get permission to move forward:

Did I catch you at a bad time?

No. It's fine. I have a minute.

Or they tell you that now is not a good time: *"When would be the best time to call you back?" "In fact, I might be able to get over there Thursday morning - would 9 or 10am be ok for you?"*

MISSION ACCOMPLISHED - we now have a Sales Platform.

If they are not the decision maker, ask for their help.

Who does facilities management for your building?

Or

I was hoping you could help me. Who would be the right person to speak to about your air conditioning equipment?

Or

Can you help me to figure out who the right person is that would know about your air conditioning equipment?

Possible Responses: (prepare an A+ response for each one)

- What is this about? *(Use this or something shorter – whatever works:*

In new construction or when replacing an air conditioning system, most builders use the cheapest air equipment because the building owners are very price sensitive - so that's how they win the bid. We install those types of low cost systems every day. Because everyone is focused on keeping the project at the lowest possible cost, the monthly electric bill is never really a consideration, but when you have to pay that bill every month, you quickly find out that the cost of energy is going up, not down. We do a quick free audit to determine how much you can save over the course of time with more efficient equipment - does that make sense?)

or shorter...

(We work with 30,000 sq. ft. and larger facilities and show them multiple ways to lower energy costs - air flow, heat isolation, state and federal rebates, things like that. Who would be the person to speak to about your air conditioning equipment?)

- Who are you again? *(You now have a sales platform. Take your time, step up to the plate and work your magic)*
- I'm the guy. *(Great. I'm talking right to the source. What air conditioning equipment do you have installed now?)*
- Our facilities engineer, but he's not here today. *(What is his name and direct number?)*
- We outsource our building management to another company. *(Great. What company, and who is your contact person there?)*
- We don't own the building. *(But you pay the electric bill right? Let me have the contact information and I can see if I can get them to consider more efficient equipment that will cut your electric bill).*
- We already have the equipment we need. *(Oh so you wouldn't be interested, I understand. What air conditioning equipment do you have installed now?)*
- We use AAAA Air Conditioning and we're happy with them. *(Oh so you already have a great relationship with AAAA, I understand. What air conditioning equipment do you have installed now?)*
- Any decisions like that are made by our purchasing manager (or CFO, Facilities Mgr., General Manager, etc.). *(Great. What is his direct number?)*
- We wouldn't be interested in anything like that. *(Oh so you wouldn't be interested. I understand. What air conditioning equipment do you have installed now?)*

RUNNING THE NUMBERS:

Assume the average proposal is $60,000 and your commission is 5%.

Let's say you make 25 cold calls. Let's say you talk to ten of them and are successful at scheduling an energy audit with three of them, and then you average a 30% close ratio on your proposals.

Obviously, the follow up calls, the audit, the proposal and the sale may take months - but these 20 cold calls will result in the following business activity:

Cold Calls Made: 25
People Reached: 10
Energy Audits Scheduled: 3
Proposals Generated: $180,000
30% Closing rate: $54,000 in sales
Commission: $2,700

Not bad for making 25 phone calls and doing the follow up. In fact, that's $2,700 more than the other salespeople who don't make cold calls.

Assume you maintain the same 30% closing rate on your proposals, but you are able to improve your cold calling skills and are able to schedule more energy audits.

Cold Calls Made: 25
People Reached: 10
Energy Audits Scheduled: 4
Proposals Generated: $240,000
30% Closing rate: $72,000 in sales
Commission: $3,600

Cold Calls Made: 25
People Reached: 10
Energy Audits Scheduled: 5
Proposals Generated: $300,000
30% Closing rate: $90,000 in sales
Commission: $4,500

If you can continue to improve your cold calling skills and get one more audit scheduled:

Cold Calls Made: 25

People Reached: 10
Energy Audits Scheduled: 6
Proposals Generated: $360,000
30% Closing rate: $108,000 in sales
Commission: $5,400

Improving your skills on the call will dramatically increase your income.

Different Types of Sales

Different types of selling situations present you with different types of Sales Platforms.

The techniques are the same, but there are differences.

Read through all the material below – even if you are engaged in a different type of sales scenario – because I include some good "nuggets" in each section.

Remember that ALL salespeople, regardless of the type of sale they are engaged in, need to understand the basic sales skills surrounding communication and influence.

Selling to Consumers in Their Home

In this type of sale you are selling one product, and one product only. You may only get one shot at a Sales Platform (one "at bat") each day. With cancelled appointments, you may not even get a shot every day.

In this type of sale you will typically be sent to an appointment. Appointment setters have done their job, but it is hit or miss that the people will even remember agreeing to the appointment. It is critical that you call and confirm the appointment before you begin driving and confirm that all decision makers will be there. Treat these appointment confirmation calls as the beginning of the sales process. You will many times get questions, and they will try to get out of the appointment. "What is it you're selling again?" "We don't really need that."

It's a tough gig, but in-home selling is a great way to really learn and master the craft of selling. You are face to face with a homeowner on their turf. You need to master every step of the process.

You will hear the same questions over and over, and of course you'll be ready for those, but you will also get some curve balls that you may not have been expecting, and this is your opportunity to handle them and hit them out of the park.

Because there is a very high level of rejection, and most days it's an "all or nothing" payday, in-home selling should only be for very experienced and self-confident sales professionals. But unfortunately, these jobs tend to go to younger, inexperienced salespeople who are allowed to shadow someone for a few days, and then they are on their own. Of course, a high rate of rejection results in a very quick exit for most, and a high turnover rate. Unfortunately, many of these younger salespeople end up leaving the profession. For salespeople who succeed in this type of environment, the sky's the limit. If you can do this, you should be able to succeed in almost any sales environment. Successful in-home salespeople have all my respect.

Parameters for this type of sale:

- Your appearance, demeanor, and body language are critical. The ability to read the demeanor and body language of the customer is critical.

- Closing skills are critical. There is no relationship. There are no proposals to consider. There is no follow-up contact. You learn to close on the first call, or you don't make any money that night.

- You only get one shot at it. When the customer says "Leave your card and we will call you" what that really means, as every in-home salesperson knows, is "NO". They are never calling you, and you are never going back to that house again.

- This type of sales situation probably requires the highest level of self-confidence because ringing someone's doorbell at night with the German Shepard barking through the crack in the front door – this is not for most people. You need a very high level of self-confidence.

- Every step of the sales process must be mastered – the introduction, putting people at ease, gaining their interest early, being able to modify your approach to different types of people, needs development, questioning skills, presentation skills, handling objections, and of course, the close.

- Memorize and perfect the "Doorknob Close" now also called the Columbo close.

When you have failed to close and you are leaving the home, when your hand touches the doorknob pause, turn back to the prospects and say these words exactly:

> *"You know, I have a problem and maybe you can help me. I'm trying to figure out something... You said you liked the product, right? You said you needed the product, right? You said the price was fair, right? Is it something I said? Or maybe something I didn't say that I should have?"*

Most of the time, they will say "No. You did a great job."

Then you say: *"Tell me what would need to exist for you to move forward on this tonight?"*

Of course you have nothing to lose, and more than half the time the conversation will open again and you get another shot.

As you gain experience in in-home sales, your closing rate should increase week to week. The Doorknob Close is a must to keep more opportunities alive.

Would you keep trying even after the prospect has said "NO"?

After the prospect has said NO, and even after they have given you a good reason for saying NO – as long as you keep the conversation going (chit chat, small talk, comments about the weather, do you know ____? I have a good friend who lives in ____) – as long as they haven't shut the door (or hung up the phone) – you have a shot to cycle through the process again (to start with a fresh sales platform) and work toward a close.

In fact, this "re-set" of the conversation (from "NO" to chit chat to starting again) often times will

change the chemistry, and you now might be viewed a friend, and the customer just might say, "You know, let's go ahead and do this." And even if that doesn't happen, your next cycle through the process will be much better received.

Selling to Consumers in a Store

Although I find it hard to believe, most retail salespeople are not trained. You can tell this because when you walk into a store they will ask "Can I help you?" Then I say, "No thanks, just browsing." See the chapter on [Impulsive Opposition](#).

In retail selling you should get many Sales Platforms, lots of "at bats," every day.

Retail selling, as opposed to in-home selling, involves multiple products and helping the customer sort through all the options. You are an advisor.

Because people are already interested in the product or service you are selling, great retail sellers have very high close rates. Normally, commissions are very small so if you want to make a decent living, you will need a retail store that drives a lot of traffic.

Here are some of the parameters for this type of sale:

- People are coming to you because they are (at least somewhat) interested. Nobody walks into a carpet store to just "browse". They are in the market for carpet.
- Your appearance, demeanor, and body language are critical.
- Through needs development questions, find out what they are looking for and begin to narrow down their choices.

Needs Development Example:

If I'm selling washing machines I'm going to ask questions like:

How many loads do you do in a week?
Do you have children?
Do you use your washing machine to clean your comforters, or do you take those to the cleaners?
Do you prefer a front load or a top load?
What color do you prefer?
Do you have a brand name that you prefer?
Have you thought through a budget?
Etc.

- "Great. Let me show you a few options which I think will meet your needs."

  "There are so many different models here, let me show you several that might fit the bill."

  "From what you've told me, these three are probably going to be the best fit for you."

- With your superior knowledge of the products, you now show them three choices (Good/Better/Best), and you explain how each feature matches to what they asked for – and in the process you can explain why the cheap ones (that you're not going to show them) will not meet their needs.

- After you have shown them three choices (Good/Better/Best), show them a better, more expensive option – the top of the line that will meet all their needs perfectly.

  We do this, obviously, because the more expensive one is significantly better than the ones they have been looking at – and because you have trained them on all the in's and out's of washing machines, they are now educated on what makes it better. They might be able to spend more money to get the more expensive option, but even if they don't it helps them come to terms with the price of

- the other units – makes it seem like they really aren't paying that much.

- Get the husband filling out the credit app while the wife asks you questions about each model.

- Know all your facts and all the common questions you are going to get asked. i.e. delivery and installation, price match guarantee, warranty, etc. If you have separated the husband and wife, and have answered all these questions for the wife – the husband will come back and ask the same questions – and now the wife can step in and answer them for you. (Now you're a pro!)

- UPSELL:

    As the conversation winds down, ask this question:

    "What else are you shopping for?"

    Move away from the washing machines – that's closed. You are now their best friend, and now it's time to upsell. Combine the washing machine with the refrigerator, then walk them to the High Definition TVs. (OK. NOW you're a pro!!!)

    "Have you seen our High Def TV's?"

    or… *"I don't know if you saw this yet, but we're having a special on _____."*

Develop several easy transition statements that move you to other items.

Selling to Businesses by Phone

You need three things to succeed in outbound business telephone sales:

- Work Ethic
- Product Knowledge
- Sales Technique

Work Ethic:

In outbound telephone sales you will most likely be situated in a sales bullpen. Be the one who makes the most outbound phone calls. Keep dialing then dial some more. Whether you won or lost on your last call, dial another number.

Unless you already have a great customer base that calls or emails orders to you all day, your success will depend to a very large extent on your outbound call volume. Keep calling and get more and more swings at it. The more potentials you talk to, the more "at bats" you're able to get, the more you can practice new sales skills and improve.

Here's a cautionary tale. I once hired a guy who, on the job he was leaving, was required to make 70 outbound phone calls a day. I told him I thought that was a lot of calls, and he told me everyone there makes that volume of calls. This guy had an almost super-human work ethic. He was always the first person in the office, and he was always there at his desk when I would leave at night. After a few weeks his sales numbers still hadn't kicked in, so I made an excuse to sit in the bullpen and do some work so I could listen to his pitch. He would call, call, call and then when he got a prospect on the phone he went into his pitch. I now understood why he wasn't making any sales. He was rushing through his pitch so fast that he didn't take any time with the customer. It almost sounded like he felt bad about interrupting them and he didn't want to take up any of their time, or that he felt he needed to hurry up and make more calls. When we got him to slow down and become a sales professional (rather than a phone dialing professional) he began to connect with his customers and build some strong sales numbers.

Dial the phone early and often, but when you do get a prospect on the phone – take your time. Laugh with them. Ask them questions. Dig deep and learn about their company and their situation. Don't short change the sales process just to reach a certain activity level. Be like the great baseball slugger who saunters into the batter's box – prepared and ready, alert to every possibility.

Make calls, leave messages, follow up on your quotes, grab new incoming leads. Even when you have achieved several good sales months in a row, get back to your work ethic. You may not be the (best, brightest, youngest, oldest, most experienced...) but you can always be the hardest working salesman in the room.

Early in my sales career I was working next to a great salesman – he was the leader every month – and one day at 4:30pm he put a $5 bill on the corner of his desk and he said "$5 says you can't make more phone calls – or more sales – than me by 5:30pm." This guy was making twice what I was making, and yet he still worked harder than anyone in the room. That's the kind of work ethic that pays off with more "at bats", more opportunities, more sales, more relationships, more of everything.

You're already at work. You might as well give it everything you've got. All the benefits from your hard work go straight to your bottom line.

Product Knowledge:

In outbound telephone sales you must have excellent product knowledge and a strong understanding of your company's internal procedures. In fact, there is no substitute for product knowledge. You may have superior sales skills, but if you don't understand the products inside and out – you will struggle against salespeople who have superior knowledge.

You are a consultant, and you must be able to gather useful information from your customers then guide them through the product options to the best solution. Product knowledge is essential.

Sales Technique:

For some reason, a lot of companies think that if you understand the product very well you can get on the phone and sell it. I have seen a lot of companies do this, and I have watched very strong engineers flounder as salespeople, and I have watched strong engineers adapt to the sales position and flourish in their new career.

Product Knowledge is critical, but it does NOT equal Sales Technique.

Selling to Corporations or Large Groups

Many salespeople deal with large purchases which need the approval of many people within a company. These sales may have a lead time of six months, a year, or even longer.

The sales cycle typically begins when you find a champion within the company. Through diligent effort you have worked your way through the company and found a person in the group who will eventually use your product or service.

This is your "Internal Champion." This person thinks your solution is great, he understands it fully, understands the benefits, and wants to proceed. He likes you and your product, and by recommending it he is pinning his reputation and possibly his career on your solution and your professionalism.

In most cases you want to personally present your solution to the next layer of decision makers – even when your champion truly believes in the solution. When the champion presents it, he is often shot down because he can't answer many of the questions which you would have been able to handle. Now the deal is soured because the next level of decision makers has a bad first impression.

Walk me through your decision process.

How can we get the next level of decision makers together so I can present this solution to them?

I will present it to them.

(Be prepared for this response and have several of your own responses prepared)

I appreciate that. What I have found is that the next level of decision makers often ask questions that my internal champions don't know how to answer, and I have found that their first impression ends up being their lasting impression. How can we get me, or perhaps my management team involved in that presentation? I want to give our solution the best possible chance of success, does that make sense?

Within a large corporation, it's critical to understand that not everyone involved in the decision has the same priorities. Someone at the table may even be the internal champion for a competing solution.

While these buying criteria relate to all types of purchase situations, many of these are very important in larger corporate environments.

Buying Criteria:

- Risk of changing vendors
- The time and hassle of changing vendors
- The time and hassle of changing procedures
- Quality
- Value
- Understanding the product
- Understanding the benefits
- Can I picture the results?
- Timing
- Budget
- Reputation of the vendor
- Warranty and service after the sale
- Do they like/trust the salesperson

Before the meeting, you need to get the lay of the land from your internal champion:

> Before this presentation, tell me a little about your internal discussions. I'm trying to find out what issues are important to the different people who will be in attendance.
>
> Who else is part of the decision process that is not going to be at this meeting?
>
> What other options are you discussing internally, and what are the strengths and weaknesses of our solution vs. the other solutions you are considering? (Remember, doing nothing is another option)

During that presentation, I always start off by acknowledging that different people in the room may have different perspectives and different priorities. The IT guy is overworked. The CFO is worried about going over budget. The CEO is considering an acquisition on the horizon which may complicate your sale.

> Before I begin, I know that each of you have different perspectives and priorities, and I'm hoping that you can share some of your needs, so when I present our solution I can make sure to cover the things that are important to each of you.

Or

> I understand John's issues pretty well – we have talked a number of times. But before I jump into my presentation I would like to hear from others in the room about your different priorities and perspectives.
>
> What other issues do I need to consider and address in my presentation?
>
> What else?
>
> That's interesting. Tell me what you mean by _____.

> *What else?*

Again, during the meeting:

> *Can you walk me through your decision process?*

Trial close questions are critical during large meetings.

> *What if You Get No Body Language or Feedback?*

> If your solution is being compared to alternative solutions, or if the people in the meeting don't know how the CEO feels about the solution, the participants are not going to give you much body language. Ask trial close questions to see how you're doing.

> *What questions do you have up to this point?*

> *How do you feel about this so far?*

> *I know you're considering alternatives – how does this compare?*

> *We talked about your priorities earlier in the meeting, how do you feel about this so far?*

> *Pick the sourest looking person: I want to make sure we have addressed your concerns. What are your thoughts so far?*

Here's a trial close question which is particularly effective in groups:

> *Do you like it?*

I know! Never ask a yes-no question. But here's why this is effective in group settings (whether it's a husband/wife, or ten Director and C level executives around a table). There are normally going to be people who are very receptive to your solution, and people who are going to reserve judgment, and even people who are championing an alternative and privately arguing against your solution.

When you come out and ask – *Do you like it?* – you are getting a lay of the land. You are also affecting the group dynamic because now everyone knows there are certain people who like your solution. Now your follow-up questions will draw even more specific information about why they like it.

Or you may hear everyone say they don't like it – and then you can agree and clarify their objections and cycle through the presentation again to address those issues.

If negative: Agree and Clarify

I hear your concerns. Tell me a little bit more about what you mean when you say...

I'm sure you have some other concerns, please don't hesitate to bring them all up right here.

If positive: Ask the follow-up questions:

Great. How does this address your priorities?

Great. Imagine after you have implemented this solution you will now have a single dashboard combining all these metrics into one location. That's going to make a big difference, won't it?

Or paraphrase: So this is going to meet your needs?

Tell me more.

Tell me more.

What else?

What else?

What is your timeframe on this project? When do you need this fully implemented? (Oh wow we will need to get started as soon as we can!)

What is your decision process?

What will be the best way for me to keep up to date on your process and be available to answer questions as they arise?

After your meeting there is a long process of internal discussions going on for weeks and months behind closed doors. During this time your sale is in the hands of several different people. Unknown to you, your future is rising and falling based on conversations you are not a part of – and depending on people you have never met.

Here's where you check in with your customer each week:

I haven't heard any news in a while.

Is there something going on that is endangering this proposal?

What are people saying about our solution?

Where is our solution looking good, and where is it not so good?

Off the record – what's going on behind the scenes?

What can we do to keep this fresh in everyone's mind?

I'd like your help. If you were me, what would you be doing to move this forward?

Let's see if we can schedule the initial site evaluation. I know you guys haven't made a formal decision, but this is free anyway, and will save about two weeks once you do.

Self-Evaluation After Every Call

I do this all the time, and I believe it is critical to review each call or situation when it's over. You may be able to call a customer back and fix something you said wrong, or ask a question you forgot to ask, but most important for me is asking myself – how did I handle that, and what will I do better next time?

> *The chemistry on that call was awful. How can I shake it up next time to get the customer to share more information?*
>
> *I had an opportunity to ask him about future projects – why didn't I?*
>
> *I heard myself talking over the customer and interrupting several times. Stop that!*
>
> *He gave you a clear objection, why did you lecture him and not ask him for more information?*
>
> *Why am I calling him back next week to wrap this up? Could I have closed it on this call?*

A good sales manager will hear you on a good call and say the following:

> *That sounded like a really good call – what's going on?*

Then the proud sales rep will tell the manager about the call and the opportunity.

Then the sales manager asks a few questions:

> *Who does he buy from now? Why is he willing to ditch them and use us?*
>
> *Will he price shop your quote with his current vendor?*

What's his timeline on this purchase?

Did you try to sell him other products?

What other projects does he have after this one?

How long has he had this job?

Etc.

And everyone in the sales room hears this. If the guy nails all the questions – that's fantastic. If not, you can be sure he will raise his game on the next one. And everyone in the sales room will raise their game.

If your manager doesn't do post-call analysis like this, then you need to analyze your own calls and look for things you did right, things you did wrong, and identify two or three things you will work on the next call.

Every time you dial the phone, or every time you go into a meeting, or every time a customer walks through the front door – you should have three things in your mind that you're going to work on during this sales call. Don't focus on the outcome – focus on improving your sales skills on every call.

How to Work a Trade Show Booth

Whenever I attend a trade show, I walk the floor and I evaluate the skill of the salespeople in the booths. In this situation, I am not a qualified buyer, I'm just walking the trade show floor and trying to learn and broaden my perspective and understanding about Sales, my favorite subject.

I usually do this floor walking late in the day when it's quiet. I don't want to take the salespeople away from their real potential customers.

I'll walk down the aisle and look at the signs in the booth, and then I approach the salesperson. "Hello. Your booth looks interesting. Tell me what you do."

Then as I listen to their pitch I evaluate their skills. I always ask a lot of questions so I can learn.

If you want to get an "A" from me when you're at your next trade show, here's what you need to do.

"Hello. Your booth looks interesting. Tell me what you do."

Your answer should be…

"Well, we actually have quite a few products/services. **Tell me a little about what you do** and then I can zero in on the products/services that will meet your needs."

Remember what we learned about Listening.

As I explain what I do, or what I'm interested in, a good salesperson will ask more and more and more questions. Let me do the talking, and then the salesperson can zoom in on possible areas of partnership, or can immediately realize that there is no match and send me on my merry way in 30 seconds rather than wasting his breath by giving me the whole pitch (which wasn't going to be relevant to me anyway).

Ask before you tell. Then ask more probe and clarify questions. Then ask more questions. Reflect, paraphrase. Then a few more, and when you feel you know enough about the customer, NOW you can begin to present your solution, or address his need.

Most salespeople never even ask a question, they just jump into their pitch. And the scary thing is, these are experienced salespeople who have been through many different training sessions. These are the sales people the company has paid to bring to the trade show.

Even after your presentation you need to know what they are thinking.

What do you think?

How does that sound?

Does that make sense?

The Trade Show "Bounce"

There are two types of trade shows, or two different reasons why you / your company is at the trade show.

Purpose One: Brand Awareness / Marketing

The first purpose of a trade show is to gain brand awareness / marketing. If you are at the trade show for this purpose, then your goal is to talk to as many people as possible. You are searching for potential partners, potential vendors or suppliers, channel partners, distributors, future customers – you may also want to spend time visiting your competitor's booths to learn more about the industry.

As people walk by your booth, try to grab everyone's attention.

Use an opening question where "yes" or "no" is a good answer. An example would be: "Have you heard about the new XYZ 1000?"

Whether they answer yes or no, you can begin to engage in conversation.

You will find that most people walk straight past your booth, avoiding eye contact. Just ask your opening question and try to pull them in.

Even for those that open their body language as they walk by – ask your opening question and engage them in conversation.

Purpose Two: Closing Sales at the Show

Many salespeople need to close business at the show. Whether it is getting a signed contract, or a credit card – they need to close business at the show in order to make money – right now.

In this case, you don't want to talk to everybody. You want to talk to the people who will buy from you today.

Suppose there are 3,000 attendees at the show. Suppose about 40% are potential customers. Then further suppose that about 30% of those people are in a position to buy today.

Of the 3,000 attendees, maybe about 300 are in a position to buy your product or service today. So your job is not to talk to 3,000 people, but to sort through the 3,000 to get to the 300 that are buying today.

Of course, when the show traffic is slow, you should talk to everyone. But when the traffic gets busy – you need to learn the "Trade Show Bounce" technique.

If they walk by without giving you body language – let them go.

If they give you body language, ask your opening question: "Have you heard about the new XYZ 1000?"

Whether they answer yes or no, you can engage them in conversation.

Then you quickly ask: "Is this something you would consider purchasing?"

If yes, continue shortly thereafter: "What is your approximate timeframe for this purchase?"

They have given us body language interest. They have told us they would consider buying your product/service, and they might consider purchasing soon. These are the people you want to spend time with.

When the show gets busy:

- If they don't give you body language – let them go.
- If they tell you they are not interested, or may be interested – Bounce to the next person walking by.
- If they tell you they are interested, but not for a few months or years – Bounce.
- If they engage in conversation, but start pointing out all the negatives of your product/service, try to overcome the objection. But if they stay negative – Bounce.
- If they trap you in a conversation about their medical history – Bounce.

Capture their information in a guest book, or by scanning their badge. By all means follow up with them after the show, but do not waste time on the people who are not buying today.

Do not get sucked into a 5 or 10 or 15 or 30 minute conversation with someone who is not going to buy today. Spend all your time locating, then working with potential buyers.

Just keep the word "Bounce" in your head. If the conversation veers off – Bounce.

You are at the show to sell today. Not to be polite, not to make friends, not for business a year from now. You are here to close business today.

Simply walk away from the person, or excuse yourself:

> "I'm the only one covering this part of the booth. I need to help those other people over there. Please sign our guest book. If you have any question, let me know."

People may say that if you spend time with some of these prospects you might be able to get them to buy today. Or if you let them go, they will buy from one of your competitors. That may be true. Who knows, maybe as many as 25% of them may buy from your competitor today. But time is the limiting factor at a trade show, and I'd rather go with the 75% odds (that they are not going to buy) than waste my time chasing the short odds (that they might buy).

Bounce, bounce, bounce. Find the buyers and engage with them. If they ain't buying, bounce.

Attitude, Hard Work and Self-Motivation

I have the worst territory

Our prices are too high

Our competition is eating our lunch

The economy is awful

I have to fill out too many reports and go to too many meetings every week

Our compensation plan is terrible

Salespeople are not treated well at this company

"You can make money or you can make excuses, but you can't make both."

—Dan Lier

"Things don't happen to you, they happen because of you."

—Grant Cardone

You must take full responsibility for your results.

It's too easy to get wrapped up in the office gripe session. I guarantee your company isn't perfect, your sales manager isn't perfect, your compensation plan isn't perfect, the economy isn't perfect, your product isn't a perfect fit for everyone, your competition is trying to take your customers from you. You already know that – now what? Complain about it, or get to work.

You must rise above it all and adopt a positive attitude.

Attitude is a choice. It's taking a different perspective. It's flipping the question in your head from dwelling on how this affects you, to taking it as a challenge and how are you going to overcome it.

Instead of trying to figure out "why this is happening," try to figure out "what can I do to turn this situation to my advantage."

Instead of trying to figure out why you lost the sale, try to figure out what you can do to win it back, or what corrections you're going to make to ensure this same thing never happens again.

When you experience a major setback or disappointment in life, or you've been wronged or lied to or cheated, it feels awful. But instead of dwelling too long on "how this is making you feel," ask yourself the question "what are you going to do to get back to where you were?"

Don't complain. Work your butt off.

This whole book is about bringing your sales skills to a new level – getting better and more skilled. But the truth is, a hard working salesman will beat a talented but lazy salesman every day.

> *"If you have the choice between working hard and working smart, choose both."*
>
> *—Unknown*

> *"The dictionary is the only place that success comes before work. Work is the key to success, and hard work can help you accomplish anything."*
>
> *—Vince Lombardi Jr.*

> *"I'm a greater believer in luck, and I find the harder I work the more I have of it."*
>
> *—Thomas Jefferson*

"Things may come to those who wait, but only the things left behind by those who hustle."

—Abraham Lincoln

"Hard work without talent is a shame, but talent without hard work is a tragedy."

—Robert Half

"Opportunity is missed by most people because it is dressed in overalls and looks like work."

—Thomas A. Edison

"Hard work doesn't guarantee success, but you have no chance without it."

— B.J. Gupta

Motivating a football team is easy. You get rid of the ones who aren't motivated.

— Lou Holz

"If you can't excel with talent, triumph with effort."

—Stephen Weinbaum

"All the so-called "secrets of success" will not work unless you do."

—Unknown

Be the salesperson in the room who sets the example by working hard and choosing not to participate in all the complaining. Sometimes there are issues that need to be addressed, but that is different than complaining, making excuses, and lowering your level of effort.

What are you doing to address the problem, and in the meantime, and more importantly, what are you doing to get beyond the problem and move forward?

How Do You Fell About Money and Success?

Success is not money. Money is not success.

Money is electromagnetic. Money is unlike anything else. Money is a unique energy, charged with emotion. No matter how much you have, you always need more – you always want more. Money is great to have, but it often brings out the worst in people. Striving for money can give you no satisfaction.

The very best advice I can give you is to not work for money. Work to be the best salesperson you can be. Work for the satisfaction of knowing that you are a professional, you're constantly improving your sales skills, and constantly working on something new. Work for the very real reward of helping your customers get the best product or service or solution for their situation.

Don't let money be your reward, let your reward be when a customer calls you back to buy something else because you took great care of him the first time.

Money is an external possession, success is an internal state of mind. Success comes from giving the best effort YOU can give, from being the best YOU can be, from achieving the most that YOU are capable of achieving.

John Wooden, the legendary UCLA basketball coach said that his father gave him two principles while he was growing up:

Don't try to be better than someone else

Always try to be the best you can.

Here are a few more of my favorite John Wooden success-related insights.

"Success comes from knowing that you did your best to become the best that you are capable of becoming."

"Don't measure yourself by what you have accomplished, but by what you should have accomplished with your ability."

"What you are as a person is far more important than what you are as a basketball player."

"Never mistake activity for achievement."

"Be prepared and be honest."

"It isn't what you do, but how you do it."

"It's the little details that are vital. Little things make big things happen."

"Failure is not fatal, but failure to change might be."

"Do not let what you cannot do interfere with what you can do."

"Success is never final; failure is never fatal. It's courage that counts."

Be YOUR Best

Don't try to catch the guy who's in first place – be the best you can be. Wherever you come out, it's ok because you gave it YOUR best.

Don't try to beat the guy who's in second place – reach for unlimited heights. Why measure yourself against the second best salesperson in the company? Achieve the very most YOU can achieve.

As it turns out, if you focus on improving and perfecting your craft, focus on working hard, focus on raising your potential and your vision to higher and higher opportunities – you will rise to the top.

Why Do People Work?

From my observations, people work for four reasons. Each person places a different value on each of these factors, but in general here is what you should be getting from your job.

Pride: being respected, being appreciated, being good at what you do

Enthusiasm: enjoying what you do, feeling like part of a team, feeling listened to

Fulfillment: feeling like this job allows you to grow and use all your skills and talent

Money: dignity, honor, self-respect, self-reliance, fulfilling your obligations to loved ones

You should consider yourself very lucky if you have a job that scores high in each of these areas.

If I was in a situation where I was making good money, but was not getting any of the other things – I'd be gone. We have all been in situations where we are not listened to, not respected, not happy, not fulfilled. Work is a trade-off. At some point, if your needs are not being met, you need to move on.

You will be best off if you work for your own fulfillment, your own enjoyment, your own pride of accomplishment. It would be great if your job gave you all those things, but where the job falls short, it's up to you to fill in the gaps.

There are some very bad sales jobs – at least for my way of thinking. But there are no perfect sales jobs either. In general, make the best of what you have where you are. Don't fall into the Grass is Always Greener syndrome where every sales job you hear about is better than the one you have. It might be, but odds are, it's probably not.

Becoming a Great Sales Manager

A good sales manager plays many roles including teacher, coach, cheerleader, taskmaster, organizer, referee, talent scout, recruiter, and of course the very unpleasant task of firing people from time to time. Sometimes it's a very high paid and rewarding role, and other times it's a very tough job because the sales manager is stuck in the middle between an upper management who may not appreciate the sales function and salespeople who are unappreciated.

To be a good sales manager you have to understand the job of a salesperson, and through that understanding, be able to provide the best environment for your salespeople to succeed. You must understand what it means to live on commission, and how commission structure influences sales behavior.

You have to fight for the best environment for your salespeople – clear all the unnecessary obstacles and distractions out of their way so they can spend more time talking, meeting, executing their sales skills, and closing – which is what they are getting paid for. However, you also have to demand and track effort from your salespeople and compliance to the policies you set.

Some salespeople need training as their top priority, others need organization, still others need to be motivated and stimulated with more challenging goals and assignments.

One very important thing that a sales manager should do is to listen to the sales team about factors that are causing them stress. What is bothering them? Why is that bothering them? Is this getting worse? What do they suggest as a solution? Are there other solutions to the problems they are experiencing?

Key Performance Indicators

You must identify and track several Key Performance Indicators (KPIs) such as number of calls made, number of meetings scheduled, number of quotes or proposals, time from quote to close, percentage of quotes closed, mistakes in orders, sales revenue, margin, etc.

Track not only the end result (all organizations track revenue), but the tasks and steps which lead to the end result.

If the sales team is meeting revenue targets, but margins are declining then at a macro level the company needs to understand why margins are declining and take steps to improve. But you as the sales manager can do your part by tracking margins as a KPI and thereby focus the sales team's attention on tracking and improving that margin number.

I believe these KPIs should be published and available to all the salespeople so they can see how they measure up against one another, and can strive to improve their numbers. I wouldn't have any problem if these KPIs were available to the whole company so they can see how the sales team is performing.

When meaningful KPIs are published, salespeople focus on improving them. When their results improve, your results improve. KPIs are critical in any management role because you can't improve it if you don't track it, and it is the natural course of events that what is tracked and emphasized will improve.

You should acknowledge and reward, not only the leading salespeople, but also the salespeople who are improving in their measured results.

What Motivates Your Salespeople?

You might be surprised to find that not all salespeople are motivated only by money. Salespeople, like all employees (like all human beings) have a range of personalities and are motivated by a number of things that have nothing to do with money such as job satisfaction, feeling like part of a team, being included in decisions, company benefits, feeling like they are using all their talents and skills. The list of what motivates people goes on and on, but it's up to the sales manager to ask this question and develop a plan that meets these underlying needs. Some people shouldn't even be in sales, and would be happier and more valuable to the company in another role. The sales manager needs to be the all knowing guide to challenge everyone to improve on a personal level, and to give them the support they need to meet those personal goals.

Competition can be a motivator. Some sales groups establish teams – Green / Orange / Blue / Red / Yellow to not only share techniques and knowledge, but to develop some fun competition throughout the month.

The Weekly Sales Meeting

The weekly sales meeting should develop a culture of recognition, teamwork, sharing, but also accountability. How can you as an individual get better? How can we as a team get better? How can the company as a whole get better? This is where we discuss this as a team.

Here is an agenda that I have used.

- Introductions of new team members.
- Hello to any remote salespeople Skyping in – make them feel like they are part of the team.
- Updates and announcements from management and other organizations within the company.
- A review of KPIs and appropriate recognition that's due, and the distribution of any spiffs or rewards that were earned.
- What KPIs are we focusing on for this coming week?

- Discussion and sharing of sales techniques. What are some techniques that worked, and what didn't work last week? If a particular salesperson had a success story, have him share what he did and why it worked.
- Barriers to performance, questions, concerns.
- Product training – at least one aspect of product training should be reviewed every week.
- New opportunities that might need discussion or assistance.

Weekly One on One's with Each Sales Rep

These meetings should address both sales performance and personal goals. Keep your notes from previous one on one's and review them. You should also be reviewing key accounts and key sales opportunities each week. Establish personal goals for the coming week, and review last week's goals. What areas do you want to improve? What have you done so far to make that happen? What can I do to help you achieve your goals?

About once a month you will want to evaluate a salesperson's performance. There are three ways to view performance:

- Result of Efforts (sales)
- Quality of Efforts (technique and ability)
- Quantity of Efforts (metrics)

You should evaluate results first. If the sales rep is performing above average, or leading the pack – ask them how you can help, how you can clear roadblocks for him/her, what you can do to support and accelerate his/her efforts.

If a salesperson is achieving average or mediocre results, focus on the quality of their technique and ability. Offer to listen to calls, coach, evaluate – get more involved in the quality of their work.

If a salesperson is under-performing – then you can look at metrics. Are they making enough phone calls? Enough visits? Enough proposals? With these under-performers you need to look at activity level and quality.

It would be insulting to a top-performing sales rep to harp on the number of phone calls they are making, or the number of quotes. That is not what they need from you – they need your help to clear obstacles that are slowing them down, they need your leadership to envision new markets for them to explore and new methods. Don't nit-pick a top salesperson on metrics – it doesn't make any sense to lower his/her sights from the highest achievements.

Only if a salesperson is under-performing do you look at their metrics and ensure that their activity level is up to par. If it's not, help them become more active. If they already are active enough, then help them with the quality of their technique and ability.

Your style has to be adaptable to the level of salesperson you're managing. One approach does not fit everyone.

Being a sales manager can be the most rewarding job, but it can also be a very frustrating job. You have to work at higher levels within the company to explain the sales function, and go to battle for your sales team. You're going to win some, and you're going to lose some. But whatever happens you can't share your problems with your team – this is your burden alone.

You must care deeply not only about the company's results, but about people and their motivations and their careers.

Salespeople fight for the customer, and while you may be pulled in many different directions, you need to care about and fight for your salespeople.

You have to be firm when you make decisions and set policy, but you also have to be a great question asker and listener.

You are the single most important factor in helping your salespeople succeed, improving retention, and improving the company's financial results.

BONUS SECTIONS

Listening: Reaching the Unconscious to Gain Positive Influence

The Conscious Mind vs. The Unconscious Mind

Body Language and Non-Verbal Communication

Listening: The Way to Reach the Unconscious and Gain Positive Influence

Suggestions and Embedded Commands

Listening

Reaching the Unconscious to Gain Positive Influence

Listening is the best way to gain positive influence over another person. It seems counter-intuitive. How could a passive skill like Listening put you in a position of influence?

Listening is The Golden Skill because it powerfully affects the other person's Limbic Brain – the seat of their Unconscious mind. When you listen to someone, they will unconsciously form a positive opinion of you and will "like you, trust you, and respect you," even though you may not have said a word.

> *I've learned that people will forget what you said, people will forget what you did, but people will never forget how you made them feel.*
>
> —Maya Angelou

LISTENING = ATTENTION & RESPECT

All of us have an unconscious NEED for Attention and Respect. We want to be noticed, respected, made to feel significant, and validated. This is a basic human need at the Limbic, unconscious level. We may say "I don't care what other people think," but unconsciously we crave attention, respect and validation. Even people who say they don't need this validation – it still feels good (to the Limbic brain) when somebody gives it to us.

Because there are so few good listeners in the world, many people go most of their lives without this basic need fulfilled. The vast majority of people tend to be 'talkers' and feel the best way to get you to like them is for them to tell you more and more about themselves. Very few people are good at just listening.

By listening you are fulfilling a person's unconscious need for Attention and Respect. In fact, there are so few good listeners in the world today, that you may be the ONLY person who is giving them Attention and Respect. At the Limbic, unconscious level when you fulfill this basic human need, you are immediately liked, trusted and respected. In fact, even if you don't say anything, the person will not only like you, but will give you credit for being "smart, intelligent, nice, wise, kind, generous, etc." People will unconsciously put you in that category, even if you have never said a word.

People also tend to like, respect, and trust people they perceive as being similar to them. This includes techniques such as mirroring tonality, mirroring body posture and gestures, and using the same accent, words and phrases as the other person. Over time, people in the same groups tend to mirror one another's speech patterns and body language unconsciously. When you come into a group and intentionally mirror their speech and body language, this often can come across as insincere, so the best advice is to simply be yourself and have people like, trust and respect you for who you are – and genuinely listen to them.

This also works in a negative way through unconscious (but often times conscious) stereotypes and prejudices where people perceive you at an unconscious level as different, not part of their group. As an example, it has taken women decades to overcome stereotypes in professional circles. There are, of course, many more examples of conscious and unconscious stereotypes and prejudices in society which prevent certain people from gaining influence. These stereotypes and prejudices may be based on race, sex, sexual orientation, age, religious beliefs, style of dress, economic status, education status, occupation, etc.

While we cannot control the prejudices of other people, we can control our own behaviors and communication techniques, and on the grand scale, **listening is by far the most powerful of all techniques** because you are not just blending in with them, you are fulfilling their Limbic need for Attention and Respect. You are nurturing the person on an unconscious level.

So why is it so difficult to listen, and how do we listen effectively?

There are several primary reasons why listening is so difficult for us.

First is that our minds can think about eight times faster than most people talk. So while someone is talking to you, you either already know what they are going to say, or your mind fills in the gaps while it waits for the next word or for the next sentence. This works the other way, too. While you are talking, your customer's mind is on everything but you – he's not really listening to you.

The second reason is that our culture values assertiveness. You believe that it's more important to get your way than it is to hear the other person's way. We have developed a lifetime of negative habits which cause us to jump in while someone else is talking, finish their sentences for them, and move them back onto our ideas.

You ask your customer a question: *"I heard you are opening a new division – what will it be?"* Great Question!

"The new division will be focused on international expansion."

To which you should then be asking more questions to get more information, but most salespeople jump in at this point, *"Our product is certified in over 70 countries, and we have international partners who provide on-site support 24/7."*

Because of our need to assert ourselves, we lose opportunity after opportunity.

The third primary reason why listening is so difficult is that it takes time to listen, and we simply don't want to give our time away. The classic example is the children come home from school and the mother or father is watching TV. The kids are excited to tell their parents all about their day at school and the parents "listen" while they are watching TV. They simply don't want to make the time to turn around, focus on their children, and show them attention and respect.

Think about your own situation, maybe at work. On Monday morning when you ask someone how was their weekend, you really don't want to know the details, do you? Listening takes time, and we are so impatient and self-centered, that we don't want to really spend the time it takes to listen.

But listening in sales is key. Aside from the information you can gather, the very act of listening affects your customer's limbic brain and gives them a strong, positive feeling toward you.

So how do we listen? What are the actual techniques to listen?

We have never been taught to listen, and we don't have any good role models that we can copy – hardly anybody is a good listener.

There are two main techniques to listening.

Pulling the Rope, and Paraphrase/Reflect.

Pulling the Rope is asking open ended questions, then following up with more open ended questions. You ask question after question after question, and imagine that you are pulling a rope while they are talking – the more they give you, the more you ask for until finally you have all the available information.

The best non-sales example of this technique is when you call in to a computer help desk.

Ok, what operating system are you using?

What was the error message?

Have you tried turning your computer off and restarting?

Can you connect to the internet?

How much memory do you have installed?

Etc.

Etc.

They gather all the possible information, then...

Ok, based on what you're telling me I have a few ideas I'd like to try. Go to Commands... etc.

As salespeople, we need to do the same thing. Gather all possible information, then...

Ok, based on what you've told me about your situation I have a few ideas that might work... etc.

Examples:

You: *"I heard you are opening a new division – what will it be?"* Great Question!

Customer: *"The new division will be focused on international expansion."*

You: *"Tell me more about that."*

Customer: *"Well it's going to focus on 1, 2, and 3."*

"Wow. What else is the new division going to focus on?"

"You mentioned that it's going to focus on 2. That's interesting. Tell me more about that."

"What prompted the company to start a new division?"

"What countries will be your primary focus?"

"When will the new service be rolling out?"

"What technology platform will the new division be using?"

You can think of a hundred questions – and then you can ask questions to clarify their answers. Like pulling a rope – gather more and more information by asking open ended questions.

What brings you into the store today?

Well, I'm thinking about buying a new tent?

Oh, what do use the tent for?

How often do you go camping?

Do you already own a tent?

What's important to you when you're out camping?

How many people does the tent need to hold?

What else, besides the tent, are you looking to upgrade?

Where do you normally go camping?

Etc.

You will recognize these as [Needs Development](#) questions. And in sales, that's what listening is about.

By listening, you gather more and more information so that you can focus your solution directly to their situation. And by continually asking open ended question, "pulling the rope," you have all the information you want.

Another great time to practice listening skills is when a customer expresses a concern or an [objection](#).

You seem uncomfortable, what are your concerns?

What else are you concerned about?

Why do you say that?

What will your boss (wife/husband/board of directors/executive team) think is the biggest concern?

These types of questions help you uncover the real reason for the objection.

The old method of hearing an objection, then turning it around and closing on the objection went out with the dinosaur. Rather than ABC Always be Closing, try ABA Always be Asking.

The second listening technique is Paraphrase/Reflect.

This is simply repeating back what they have just said. It is a Green Light which allows them to say more.

Where are you from?
I'm from Minneapolis.
Reflect: *Minneapolis?*
Paraphrase: *Wow, you're from Minnesota?*
Open Ended Question: *Wow. Tell me more about Minneapolis! Or What's it like in Minneapolis?*

Either way, they will tell you more.

We're opening up a new division.
Reflect: *A new division?*
Paraphrase: *Wow, you're expanding?*
Open Ended Question: *Tell me more about the new division. Or What is the focus of the new division?*

How was your day honey?
Exhausting.
Reflect: *Exhausting?*
Paraphrase: *Wow, so you had a rough day?*
Open Ended Question: *Wow, what happened? Or Tell me about it, I'm listening.*

Here's how this conversation usually goes. We simply don't listen.

How was your day honey?

Exhausting.

You think you had a rough day? We had four clients visit the office today, and we had to get this ridiculous proposal out before 5pm, and my biggest customer cancelled his order.

Listening is the one skill that transcends "what you do" and actually gets to the core of "who you are" as a person. Even more importantly, it allows you to define "who you want to be" to the people who matter most in your life.

It is the single communication skill that transcends your job and works for you on a personal level to build and strengthen relationships.

Also, because so few people are good listeners, you can easily differentiate yourself from all other salespeople. If you do listen to your customers, you actually are different than all other salespeople.

The Conscious Mind vs. The Unconscious Mind

The most powerful communication techniques are designed to bypass the Conscious mind and reach a person's Unconscious mind.

The brain is divided into two parts. The cortex is the folded part of the brain and is associated with your Conscious mind. The limbic, or brain stem, is associated with your Unconscious mind.

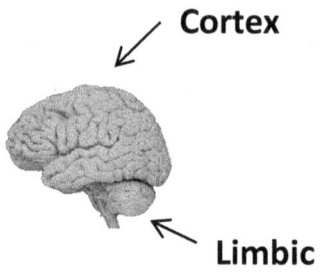

The Conscious mind is responsible for creating words and analyzing everything that enters its awareness. The Conscious mind concerns itself with all inputs from the five senses, and attempts to tie together the past, present and future into a giant ongoing analysis. It is constantly analyzing the current situation, analyzing the past, and predicting the future. The Conscious mind is obsessed with knowing and figuring things out, past, present, and future. The Conscious mind never stops chattering from the instant you wake up to the instant you fall asleep. As long as you're awake, it never stops chattering.

The Unconscious mind, associated with the limbic brain, works completely differently. The Unconscious mind operates based on emotions and impulses. ***The Unconscious mind feels rather than thinks, and is therefore much more susceptible to influence.***

The Unconscious mind operates for the most part beneath our conscious awareness. Like, dislike, trust, mistrust, superiority, inferiority, stress, fear, frustration, anger, love, sexual desire, hurt, happiness – all emotions originate in the Unconscious, limbic, mind.

Even though these feelings are unconscious, they are extremely important. The Unconscious mind affects us all day, prompting us to take action, make decisions, like or dislike an experience or a person, trust or mistrust a person, feel confident or insecure, feel attraction or avoidance – and we don't know why – it affects us unconsciously, without being aware that it is even happening.

Advertisers speak directly to your Unconscious mind all the time. I can give you a hundred logical reasons why you should like this car – some people will be swayed by my logical arguments, others will still not like the car. But if I place attractive people next to the car – you like the car – and you're not even aware that you like the car – and you don't know why you like the car. This is why advertisers use attractive women to sell anything from cars to beer to makeup to vacation destinations.

Advertisers use suggestive images to bypass the logical Conscious mind and speak directly to the limbic brain, to the Unconscious mind, because they know that your Unconscious mind directly influences your emotions, your behavior and your decisions all the time, and you don't even know it.

Key Point to Remember:

Effective Communication is Targeted to the Unconscious Mind

Most people think about communication as talking, explaining something or convincing someone to their point of view. The truth about communication, and what all great communicators understand either explicitly or intuitively, is that the most effective communication is aimed at the Unconscious mind.

Appeals to a person's Conscious mind (logic and reason) work sometimes, but any parent who has tried to reason with a five year old to get him to bed understands that appeals to logic and reason don't always work. Far more effective is to reach the child's Unconscious mind and influence, suggest, motivate, persuade at an unconscious level.

Salespeople know that even if a product or service is perfect for a customer, the customer will show a natural (unconscious) resistance. If the salesperson is able to reach the customer's Unconscious mind, the customer is much more receptive to the message, and the sale then proceeds easily from step to step.

Body Language and Non-Verbal Communication

Nonverbal communication is almost always unconscious. We emote nonverbal cues all the time and they just happen. We don't think about them, and unless we have very specific training, we have no ability to control them. Think about students in a boring lecture, and then the professor says "we're almost done" every student perks up and leans forward. It's an unconscious response, and we have hundreds of these unconscious responses each day.

In 1872 Charles Darwin published *The Expression of the Emotions in Man and Animals*, and since that time science has been studying and categorizing all aspects of nonverbal communication.

There are eight general areas of nonverbal communication.

1. Facial Expression
   Smiles, frowns, rolling the eyes, eyebrow raising, lip pursing – there are hundreds of facial expressions we use every day to reflect happiness, sadness, fear, anger, boredom, lack of interest, frustration, etc.

2. Gestures
   Waving, pointing, hand signals, playing with a pen, shrugs, head nods, foot tapping – all indicate a state of mind.

3. Altering Tone/Pitch/Volume of speech
   You can say the same words in countless different ways by varying emphasis, tone, pauses, etc. This is why being

in the courtroom is so much more interesting than just reading the transcript, because so much information is transmitted with the voice in addition to the words.

4. Body Language and Posture
   Body language can be studied for a lifetime, but here is the most important thing to know about body language – space and security.

   Space: When we take up more space – chest out, arms wide, eyes up – we project confidence. When we shrink ourselves down – shoulders down, eyes down, arms and legs crossed – we project a lack of confidence.

   Security: When we open our 'soft spots' such as throat, chest, groin – we project confidence by unconsciously showing that we do not feel any threat.
   When we cover our soft spots we are unconsciously projecting a sense of insecurity, we feel threatened and are protecting ourselves.

5. Eye Gaze
   Looking, staring, blinking can all be analyzed. Research shows that when you see or hear something you like or agree with, your pupils dilate and blink rate increases. Police can often tell when a person is lying by their gaze upward and away.

   Gazing can be a sign of confidence (or staring can be a sign of aggression) while the inability to hold eye contact can be interpreted as lack of confidence.

6. Use of Personal Space
   In our culture the normal speaking distance is between 18 inches and four feet. Some cultures come 'nose to nose' when speaking. Moving in closer or moving out further than your norm sends unconscious signals which

can relate to your level of comfort, trust, power, intimacy or aggression.

7. Touch
   Some people love to hug and touch, while others avoid touching. Together with personal space, expert communicators can control and manipulate your mood and receptivity by controlling space.

8. Clothing and Appearance / Grooming
   Clothing, uniforms, hairstyle, tattoos – when you see a person for the first time you immediately form very strong unconscious opinions. While fashions have come and gone for thousands of years, clothing, costumes, uniforms, hair styles have always been used to project a message.

Becoming aware of and using nonverbal communication works both ways.

By appreciating the nonverbal cues that others are sending, you can read a person's level of interest and whether they trust you or not, and then you can modify your message accordingly.

By observing your own nonverbal cues, you can modify and control the way you come across to others, and thereby gain more trust and likability.

Master communicators use nonverbal communication to strengthen their message and get people to pay more close attention.

If you enjoy watching Cesar Milan "The Dog Whisperer", then you know that all his communication with dogs is through body language: posture, facial expression, personal space, eye gaze, touch. He communicates with the dogs entirely non-verbally. Of course, dogs don't understand a word you say – their language is entirely non-verbal.

Circumstances That Influence

It would be ideal if humans made their decisions based on the facts. The reality is that we are influenced by many other factors, none of which have to do with the facts. If you watch TV ads, you will almost always see one of these factors used to influence.

As we review these influencing factors, realize that many salespeople naturally use these techniques. One by one, find different ways to weave these factors into your sales behavior. Even business people who consider all the facts and analysis end up making decisions based on one or more of the factors below, and they are unaware they are doing it.

You want to be strong on facts and analysis, but when you can find a way to add these influencing factors you will find yourself closing more deals.

1. **Reciprocity**

    If I invite you to lunch and I pick up the check, you are very likely to invite me to lunch and I would be very surprised if you did not offer to pick up the check. I do something for you, and human nature makes you feel an obligation to do something for me.

    In the old days the stereotypical salesman would use this technique: "I'll tell you what I'm gonna do. Because you're such a nice family / because you're a smart young man / because you're a pretty young lady I'm gonna give you a special deal. I'm gonna throw in ....."

    We don't have to be like the old time salesman, but we do this naturally when we say things like:

"I'll tell you what – let me see if I can get you free shipping on this, ok?"

"Let me see if I can extend the sale price for another few days. OK?"

"I'm going to go through the inventory and pick out the best one for you."

"I'll make sure your order is processed right away."

"I'll hold this here for you for another day."

"I'll keep this quote open for an extra week."

We do something for the customer – and it doesn't have to be a huge something – and the customer is influenced to do something for us – in this case do business with us.

This principle has been scientifically tested and proven with an experiment published in the Journal of Applied Psychology.

When a restaurant server leaves a mint with the bill, the average tip increases 3%.

When the server leaves two mints, the average tip increases 14%.

When the server leaves one mint, then makes a return trip and leaves a second mint "just for you" the average tip increases 23%.

2. **Authority**
"JD Powers ranked this car #1 in Customer Satisfaction"
"Vote for Jones – the only candidate endorsed by the local Police and Fire Department"
"Microsoft Certified Engineers"
"Kid tested, mother approved"
When we reference an external, third party authority we are influencing the customer's perception of our product

or service. It's not me saying it, it's this recognized third party authority.

Another use of this principle is the use of uniforms. People have a subconscious respect for uniformed authority figures. They tend to cooperate and comply with authority figures.

The most important use of this principle is your own expertise. If you are indeed an expert, if your company is truly the leader in the market, then you are a respected authority with your customers, and that is a valuable position to have.

3. **Consensus**

   "Everybody is signing up for this."

   "Three people on this block have already bought this."

   "We have been working with many companies in your same situation."

   When you can show a customer that the world is moving in this direction, they are influenced to join the trend.

   It's important to show them that customers in a similar situation have made this decision. It doesn't do any good to show them customers in another industry or with completely different circumstances and needs. They need to see that the consensus applies to them.

4. **Scarcity**

   Human nature makes us want what we can't have.

   "There is only room for three ads on the home page – and I want to make sure you get one of them."

   "The sale ends Friday."

   "We only have a few left."

   "This price is good only until our inventory is gone."

   "Year end clearance."

   If it's true – use it to your advantage. If it's not true then you will come across as fake.

5. **Liking**

   It's obvious, but people tend to buy from people they like. If, for some reason, they don't like you or don't' trust you – they are much less likely to buy from you.

   At a restaurant, if you like your server you will tend to give them a bigger tip. A server's genuine and outgoing smile will influence your tip. If they are not friendly, or overly friendly and 'not your type' you are likely to give them a minimal tip.

   In business situations we look for commonality. Oh you like to golf? Oh you went to University of Somewhere – I have a cousin who went there. Oh you're originally from Elkville, I used to go there often on business. Etc.

   Complimenting a person is another way to get them to like you. Some retail chains train their staff to approach a customer with a compliment rather than a question. It has the effect of immediately getting the person to like you – to think you are a nice person.

   The best way to get people to like you is to LISTEN to them. Ask questions, and genuinely listen to their answers. Listening reaches a person's subconscious mind and makes them feel respected and appreciated. Listening is the best way to give a person genuine respect, and of course if you respect them – they automatically have a high opinion of you.

6. **EMOTION**

   Emotion is the biggest influence factor. In the chapter on Features vs. Benefits we learned how to turn a feature (a fact) into a benefit (an emotional reason to buy). Examples:

   Fact/Feature: *The tread on these tires is a V-Shaped asymmetrical lateral groove.*

Benefit/Emotional Appeal: *That's important because that groove design allows the maximum amount of water to flow through, so when you're driving on a rainy day, your tires are touching the road surface rather than hydroplaning or sliding on the water. This groove design is more expensive because it costs more to make those intricate groove designs in the tire, but these are the safest tires available, and that level of safety is worth a few extra dollars, isn't it (especially for your wife / daughter / son who will be away at college)?*

Fact/Feature: *This game is designed with 64 bit CGI graphics and 256 color design. It is the result of the work of a team of 125 designers over three years. It is compatible with multiple game consoles.*

Benefit/Emotional Appeal: *This game ROCKS. The graphics will blow you away. You gotta get this game dude!*

As a salesperson you need to balance your approach. If you are all facts and figures and flowcharts, you need to add enthusiasm and emotion into your skill set. And vice versa, if you're all enthusiasm and outgoing personality, you need to add facts and logic into your skill set. You need to do this because everybody is different. Each person is interested in and motivated by a different feature/benefit. Each person has different priorities and different values.

Emotional appeals can include status and prestige, saving money, safety, making a 'wise' decision, impressing your spouse, job security, or just about anything else.

As you grow your sales skills you will include all these influencing techniques plus the many others presented throughout this book. In a very real sense, you are becoming a master of communication and influence, a master of words and phrases.

Words That Influence

Let's continue with more ideas which will improve your influence skills.

There are actually certain words which cause a person to pay more attention or focus on what you are saying.

The Person's Name

There are many studies which show that people actually lean forward, smile, pay attention when they hear their name. Hearing your own name actually triggers a certain part of your brain with more activity.

You want to say the person's name once in the beginning of the conversation, and then surprise them that you remember their name again at the end of the conversation.

"John, I really appreciate the opportunity to talk to you today. I know you have some important decisions ahead of you and I wanted to find out more about.... // ....John, it was really a pleasure meeting you. What are some of the next steps that you'd like to see? Great. If we can get that done do we have a deal?"

Don't over-use a person's name. Over-using a person's name is actually worse than not using their name or even forgetting their name. It is downright annoying:

"John, thank you for agreeing to meet today. John, tell me more about your needs. John, our product is going to be a perfect fit. John, as you can see..."

Because

This is a great word to add into your every day conversations when making statements or suggestions. By adding "because", you are not only suggesting a course of action, you are giving them a concrete reason why they should do it, and it gives them something specific they can agree with rather than keeping your suggestion open ended.

> "People that buy this also buy that because..."
>
> "You should probably get an extra one because..."
>
> "You should get this fixed immediately because..."
>
> "It's a good time to upgrade because..."
>
> "You might want to consider making a down payment soon because..."
>
> "Based on what you told me earlier, this is going to be a great fit because..."
>
> "I would recommend the M2000 over the M1000 because it has more..."
>
> "The Gold package is going to be perfect for you because..."
>
> "It's time to brush your teeth."
>
> "It's time to brush your teeth because you don't want to have any more cavities, do you?"

This is an easy one to try yourself and you can see the results. By adding a simple reason to support your suggestion, it gives you an opportunity to add [implicit agreement questions](#) or [loss statements](#).

> "It's time to go to bed now." (adding an implicit agreement question)
>
> "It's time to go to bed now because we need to get an early start tomorrow, remember?"

(adding a loss statement)

"It's time to go to bed now because I don't want you to lose your breakfast treat tomorrow."

Surprise

This word, like no other, immediately captures a person's complete, 100% attention.

"I've got a little surprise for you."

"I added something I know you're going to like – you'll be surprised."

"You will be surprised to hear what I found out."

"You might be surprised to hear what other customers have said about the M2000."

Imagine

In the chapter on [Future Tense](#) we talk in more detail about how to build a picture in the customer's mind so they can experience the benefits in the future.

The word "imagine" instantly focuses a person's mind on your next suggestion.

"Imagine the next time you're out shopping with your husband."

"Imagine this TV in your living room."

"Imagine three blue elephants on your front lawn."

"Imagine how much time this is going to save."

"Imagine the increase in productivity when you install this software."

"Imagine the improvement in quality when this project is completed."

"I don't know if you can see into the future, but imagine how good you are going to feel after a few weeks."

You are in control

Allowing others to feel that they control the situation is a very powerful way to influence their thinking and actions. This entire approach is expanded in great detail in the chapter A Disarming Sales Approach.

In the meantime, recognize that disarming people by allowing them to control their own destiny, to make their own decisions, is a powerful way to influence, and it separates you from the typical salespeople who try to push or convince.

Suggestions and Embedded Commands

Suggestions (also referred to as Commands or Embedded Commands) are the hidden tool that Master Communicators use every day. When you notice them, suggestions are obvious, but even if you notice them, they still have hidden effect. Suggestions target both the Conscious and Unconscious Minds.

Suggestions will work even if you have not built influence, but if you take the time to build influence through listening, validating, questioning, helping, consulting, etc. the power of your suggestions will be multiplied because they like you, respect you, and trust you and unconsciously want to do what you ask them to do.

We discussed how the Conscious mind is constantly and instantly analyzing every input. Our Conscious mind can process information about 15 to 20 times faster than our rate of speech. Therefore, when the Conscious mind is listening, there is a lot of dead time between words. During this dead time the Conscious mind is analyzing and instantly forms pictures.

So if I tell you, "I went to the circus yesterday," you may picture a big circus tent. If I continue, "I went to the circus yesterday with my wife and children," you now picture me at the circus with my wife and at least two children – your Conscious mind instantly builds a picture to match the details. "We saw five clowns and two giant elephants in the center ring. The acrobats on the flying trapeze were amazing."

At the very instant I say the words, or as you are reading the words, your Conscious mind forms pictures, and there are some vivid pictures in my description of the circus.

You've heard the example: "Don't think of the planes crashing into the World Trade Center towers."

Now you understand why you immediately think of the planes crashing into the World Trade Center towers – your Conscious mind has already formed the picture. As the individual words hit your mind, you instantaneously form the picture of the planes crashing into the towers. Your mind will later try to rationalize the fact that you're not supposed to think about it, but it always forms the pictures first, and the pictures stay in your mind.

Suggestions are conscious statements which are heard by the Conscious mind, stored in the Unconscious, and then acted upon either immediately or at a future time.

Example of a Suggestion / Command / Embedded Command

When I post a video on YouTube I sometimes include a suggestion at the beginning of the video. "**Watch to the end of this video,** and you will learn blah blah blah."

A lot of people will simply cooperate – OK I'll watch this video to the end, and they will simply comply with the suggestion.

This is referred to as a suggestion, or a command, or an embedded command.

Suggestions, Commands, Embedded Commands are really the same thing, but you will see them referred to differently. When a suggestion is preceded by other words it is referred to as an Embedded Command.

The example above is an embedded command.

Here are more examples of embedded commands.

If _____ is important to you, then **watch to the end of this video**.

You might want to **watch to the end of this video** to get all the information you need.

Don't **watch to the end of this video** if you don't care about _____.

Imagine if you **watch to the end of this video**, how much more you will know about _____.

Some people **watch to the end of this video** and get the full benefit of _____.

I'm wondering if you will **watch to the end of this video** or not.

You might want to **watch to the end of this video**.

I wouldn't tell you to **watch to the end of this video**, if I didn't think it would help you.

You may or may not **watch to the end of this video**.

Etc.

The words you wrap around the command are not important. It's not important if you suggest they do it, or not do it because, as we discussed earlier, the Mind has already formed the picture of doing it.

What's important is the command itself. The command is what gets through to the Unconscious mind.

Your pace and tone of voice is critical in delivering these commands. Slow down and drop your voice at the end of the command. "You may or may not (slower for the command) watch to the end of this video" (downward inflection – it's a command, not a question).

When using this technique in person you can reinforce the command with a hand gesture or a smile or a tilt of your head.

For example, if you are in a job interview you would say...

"If you **hire me for this job** (say it slowly, and here you can lay your hand on the desk and maybe tilt your head forward), I will be able to work with new clients to...."

"What is the next step if you **hire me for this job**." (say this as a command, not a question – and again lay your hand on the desk to mark the statement to the listener's Unconscious mind).

The interviewer always asks – "Do you have any questions for me?" I sure do!

"I notice that you are growing into new markets. Assuming you **hire me for this job** what would be my primary responsibilities?" (say the command slowly and lay your palm on the desk and tilt your head forward)

"What will I need to provide before you **hire me for this job**." (slowly, palm on the desk, etc.).

Another approach on a job interview you can mix in with these embedded commands is a repetitive phrase such as **great decision**. Not a command, but a positive phrase.

"You would be making a **great decision** if you hire me."

"I think the company made a **great decision** expanding into the European market."

"It turned out to be a **great decision** when I transferred into marketing on my last job."

Again, you want to separate this phrase from the rest of the sentence by slowing down when you say the phrase, and adding a gesture or head tilt to mark the phrase to the listener's Unconscious mind.

It looks and sounds so obvious, but rest assured 99% of people are not aware of embedded commands and they don't notice anything out of the ordinary. In fact, you will come across as confident.

Listen carefully to TV commercials and you will realize just how many embedded commands you receive in a day. When you are in person (or on a telephone conversation) these commands are even more powerful.

People are suggestible, and they want to cooperate with you. Perhaps this has happened to you. You walk into a home or an office and the person says "Shake that snow off your coat," but your first heard the word "shake" and you reflexively reached your hand out to shake. People, all of us, are very suggestible.

Time Pre-Supposition

You can create suggestions and commands which make it seem like it has already happened.

Great salespeople do this all the time.

"Imagine how good you will feel when you **buy this car** and pull into your driveway tonight."

"What will be your husband's reaction when he sees that you **bought this _____** for him?"

"Imagine after you **buy this software**. You own the software, and now you can log into the software and you have a single interface to control all your _____."

"Imagine the impression you are making as you walk into that dinner reception wearing this dress. And those shoes!"

Great coaches use this technique.

To get the best effort from their players...

"When you look back on today's game you will realize that you **put in your best effort ever**."

To recruit...

"Son – picture yourself on game day next year running out of that tunnel wearing the Gold and Black surrounded by your teammates – some of them the best friends you will ever have. Now can you see yourself here at this school?"

Great parents use this technique.

"Imagine how great that ice cream is going to taste after you put away these toys."

Let's combine a few techniques…

"Can you imagine how easy it will be to set up your Accounting spreadsheets after you **buy this software**? It feels good to finally have the right solution, doesn't it?"

"It's a perfect fit for you needs, isn't it?"

"This was a great decision, wasn't it?"

Work hard at your profession and prosper!

Alan Gordon
2018

Final Thoughts

Thank You For purchasing and reading this Book!

I hope the tips, techniques, and resources I've shared in this book got you excited about your career in Sales! The best part is, everything you need to grow and expand your powerful Sales career is now in your hands.

You can visit our website for more great tips and techniques, plus other sales products.

If you found some helpful tips and techniques in this book I would greatly appreciate your book review on Amazon. Reviews are the lifeblood of any book on Amazon and especially for the independent author.

It is my sincere hope that you will take the powerful information contained in the book and build your confidence as a salesperson and have an amazing sales career. You deserve success!

As a reward for trusting me and buying this book I also have a Free Gift For You.

Get a free one month membership in our Big Book of Sales online community! Inside this membership you will find lots of free goodies and some really helpful videos and tools. Enjoy!

To grab your reward and take a look at some of our video training courses just CLICK HERE or visit https://www.bigbookofsales.com.

If you would like to buy this book in bulk for your entire sales team, or would like sales training customized for your company, please email specialrequest@bigbookofsales.com.

Thanks!

www.ingramcontent.com/pod-product-compliance
Lightning Source LLC
Chambersburg PA
CBHW052309220526
45472CB00001B/40